The Lawman

THE LAWMAN

An Autobiography

Denis Law with Bernard Bale
With a Foreword by Rod Stewart

André Deutsch

First published in 1999 by
André Deutsch Limited
76 Dean Street
London WIV 5HA
www.vci.co.uk

A catalogue record for this book is available from the British Library

ISBN 0 233 99556 0

Typeset by Derek Doyle & Associates
Mold, Flintshire
Printed in England by MPG Books Ltd,
Bodmin Cornwall

CONTENTS

FOREWORD
by Rod Stewart

The occasion – 15 April 1967 at Wembley, England v Scotland. Denis Law slots the ball past the spread-eagled Banks. Clenched fist aloft in a salute to the masses of Scots supporters on the terraces. Scotland are one-up against their old enemy and the current world champions. The stadium erupts. Scotland were victorious that day, 3–2 the final tally.

That was my first vivid memory of the Lawman. Ever since that wonderful day whenever I turn up to play I often find myself mimicking Denis. The only difference being I can't seem to find the back of the net with quite the frequency Denis did in his heyday. Nevertheless I still thrust an arm skyward even for a humble throw-in or a corner kick and I insist on wearing the No 10 jersey (long sleeves of course). My pseudonym in hotels around the world for many years has been Denis Law. For obvious reasons that will all have to change now. So I am honoured to write these few words for one of the greatest Scottish players of all time.

I first met Denis in the Old Trafford dressing rooms after he had sustained an injury and was taken off against Leeds in the early seventies. I shuffled in to say hello and was immediately mocked by Denis for the size of my hooter. I quickly replied with rapier wit, 'That's hardly a little button in the middle of your face, mate.' And we have been best friends ever since.

Denis was one of the most stylish players to grace the beautiful game we all love but more importantly he's one hell of a good bloke. Your round, Denis!

1

KIPPER BOXES

Step off the train at Aberdeen a few decades ago and the first thing you would notice would be the unique fragrance of a fishing port. Sadly the fishing industry is no longer what it once was, but Aberdeen has a lot more going for it than sending out trawlers. However, as a boy, I grew up surrounded by kipper boxes and, but for one thing, I would probably have joined those iron men who put their lives at risk week in and week out just to ensure that fine British tradition of fish and chips remained of the highest standard.

What was that one thing? Football talent?

You must be joking. No, that one thing was fear. One trip out on a boat with my dad when I was a lad was quite enough to develop my great love for dry land. On that particular day, as far as I was concerned the sea was not simply boisterous but reminded me of something I had heard before – 'a tempestuous tormentor that would turn you the colour of a pasture, wrench your stomach inside out and beat you up unmercifully'.

It was when I saw my father standing there, quite at ease, with a smile on his face saying, 'Isn't this nice, the sea being so calm for you today?' that I realized that the ocean and I were destined to remain very distant acquaintances. There was no way I would contemplate a career in the fishing industry, and that could make life a little awkward for a lad who was born and brought up in Aberdeen where, at that time, anything other than fishing seemed almost blasphemy.

I was born on 24 February 1940 at 6 Printfield Terrace, Woodside, Aberdeen. There was no trip to the local maternity hospital for my mother. She had already had three boys and three girls and she knew what she was about. Anyway, in our tenement block there were another 29 families so there was no shortage of help or advice. It must have been a successful birth, otherwise I would not have been writing this book, but my mother and father must have wondered why they had bothered when they saw the skinny little kid they had brought into the world.

My father had been in the fishing business all his life and took time out only to serve in the two world wars. In the first he was in the army, but in the second he was a navy man. I don't remember too much about the Second World War because I was struggling to fight my way out of nappies at the time. I have a vague memory of an air-raid shelter to which I was carried by one of my sisters when the Luftwaffe decided to target the very nerve centre of the fish and chip business.

It wasn't funny at the time of course, far from it. As a child I remember the community spirit that existed in our block, which was a reflection of Aberdeen as a whole. It wasn't just the war. It was the fact that the men were away most of the time and their wives and children were never sure if their farewells would be the last. It was a threat that was constantly in the air, even before the war, and therefore the people of Aberdeen were always there for each other. It was a community made up mostly of women and children with husbands and fathers seeming to adopt the role of welcome visitors.

There was another binding influence on the community too – poverty. Yes, it's true, the men were working, but the rewards were not so high in those days and families were much larger, with many more mouths to feed. Our tenement block was council-owned and the thought of buying a house probably never even entered the heads of most people. It was quite satisfying enough to succeed in surviving without getting over-ambitious.

What was the poverty like? Nowadays for many people poverty is having to go without a holiday, having to add up as they go round the supermarket, getting in a bit of a sweat over the bills. Poverty in Aberdeen during the 1940s was being unable to put shoes on your children's feet, whatever the job paid. Most Aberdeen families, and certainly those living in our neighbourhood, were in the same position and that is why poverty brought about such a bond. Everyone shared the same struggle as those around them and helped each other where they could. It was a totally different world from the one we live in today.

It was possible in those days for people with low incomes to receive free school meals and free boots. My mother was a proud woman, however, and would not apply for what she considered to be handouts. She preferred to face the hardships with her family and friends rather than be subjected to the indignity of holding her hand out to the welfare authorities. She was right, and even though it might have made life a little easier, I am glad that she felt that way.

There was a big occasion for me when I was 14. I received my first pair of real shoes. Up to that time I had lived in plimsolls. They were great in the summer of course, but going to school during the winter when the snow was often several feet deep was not so much fun. We were allowed to take off our shoes and socks when we got to school and mine would steam on the radiator until they were baked dry ready for the journey home.

If the picture that I am painting is a depressing one, don't let it be. We were a really happy family. As the youngest, I was usually in the middle of any fuss that was going on. My older brothers, George, Joe and John, introduced me to kicking a ball, while my sisters, Ruby, Frances and Georgina, used to mother me. We knew nothing other than the life we led and we were happy and content with our lot. I still marvel at how my parents were able to bring us all up on just those few pounds a week, but they did. Mind you, I soon developed a hatred for soup and, even today, it is among my least favourite dishes.

Television was something else which we had heard about but had never seen. We were radio people, like most others, and I have to say that I still have a love for quality radio today, certainly in preference to much of the junk that we seem to be force-fed by many television companies. We had a lot of other recreational pursuits too, and football was high on that list.

Although we followed the fortunes of Aberdeen, who had a strong side during the 1940s and early 1950s, we did not often go to see them because we were much too busy playing football ourselves. In fact, if I watched football at all it would be a junior game involving my brothers. George was a good player and he would probably have made it as a pro but for breaking a leg when he was 18. He was sidelined for too long and his chances of a career in the game slipped away. He eventually went into the paper industry.

As soon as I discovered what the game was about I became football daft. I would trot to school kicking a ball against the walls as I went. I would arrive early enough for a game before we started lessons. There would be another during the morning break and again at dinner time and in the afternoon break. After school I used to rush home, do whatever I was asked and then go out for another game of football. My mother never minded me being out playing football. When you consider how small our home was, and that there were nine of us living there when father was home from the sea, you can imagine that the more bodies were outside doing something the better it was for the others.

I developed one training technique that I could put into practice within the confines of our small kitchen. Though it was mostly crowded by the gas cooker, sink and table around which we sat for our meals, overhead there was a rack hanging from the ceiling on which the laundry was aired. When meal

4

time was over I used to help clear away and hang a large ball of wool from the rack. Then, for the next few hours, I would practise heading, juggling and kicking in the kitchen. Because the rack could be raised or lowered by means of a pulley it proved to be a very useful piece of equipment.

With everyone spending so much time playing the game the standard of school football was very high and I am convinced that there were many youngsters who could have made it as professionals if only someone had spotted them. The professional game was very different then of course. Today it is an extremely rewarding profession. The prospect of earning tens of thousands of pounds each week has been a great motivation, not only for young boys but for their parents, their teachers and anyone else who comes into contact with them. When I was a boy, being a professional footballer was good from the point of view that you could get paid for doing something you enjoyed so much – not to mention the added prospect of glory in the form of medals or a Scotland shirt – but there was no way it was going to set you up for life. The pay of professional footballers was not even close to what it is today, and yet attendances were much larger and, dare I say it, the standard of play was much better too.

Very few of the lads of my acquaintance had any ambition to become professional footballers. As for me, the idea never once entered my head. Oh yes, from the very start I loved the game, but to me it was just fun and I never considered that it would eventually play such an important part in my life, even though I was quite good at it.

It was at Hilton Primary School that I had my first taste of properly organized football. I was just nine years old at the time and I was selected to play for the under-11s team. That presented a major problem because I had no boots and there was not the slightest chance that my mother could afford to buy me some – even second-hand. My mate from next door, George Geddis, came to the rescue. George had suggested that I should be picked for the team, and he proved his friendship even further when he provided me with my first pair of football boots. His mother had scraped enough money together to get him a new pair and he gave me his old ones. That gesture set me on the road that I have since travelled. If I had not been given those boots by George Geddis I might not have played for Hilton and, perhaps, the whole Denis Law story might have been very different. I have always been grateful to George for proving to be such a real pal.

Before I moved on to secondary school I spent a year at Kittybrewster School and played for their team. My confidence soared because at both Hilton and Kittybrewster I played for successful sides, and there is nothing like winning to make you feel good.

I was extremely fortunate to have such an understanding mother who helped me on more than one occasion. The first time was after I had sat my 11-plus examination and passed. My 'reward' was a place at the local grammar school. My parents were immensely proud of me because I was the first of their offspring to be offered a place at a grammar school. You can imagine how they felt when I told them that I did not want to go there.

The truth is that I had discovered, to my infinite horror, that the grammar school did not play football. At first I thought my mates were pulling my leg when they told me, but then I found out that it was true. Life at a school which excelled in rugby and cricket was no good to me. I wanted my football. My mother proved to be a real trouper when I broke the news. She wrote to my school and even went to see the headmaster and told him that she would have problems with the expense of school uniforms, rugby and cricket gear, and that I would probably be happier at a school where I could play football. He listened to all this in mild disbelief that anyone would want to pass up such a great opportunity just so that they could continue to play football, but he finally gave in and I was allocated a place at Powis Secondary Modern School.

I was quite good at technical drawing and the possibility of a career as an architect began to take shape – but that was in years to come and, for the moment, I was happy to do my best at my studies while my real enthusiasm was kept for the various school football activities.

During my first year at secondary school I was selected to play for the Aberdeen Schools' under-12 side, and I stayed in the team right through to the final of the schoolboys' cup, which was to be played over two legs against Motherwell and Wishaw. To my delight we played the away leg at Fir Park Stadium, the home of Motherwell Football Club. It was my first experience of playing on a League ground and I was thrilled by everything from the moment we arrived. We were using real dressing-rooms, a real pitch, and there were real showers. It was an experience that registered very deeply within me and, even though I still had no inkling that I might one day become a professional footballer, I am sure that first game on a major ground had an effect on my subconscious. We lost the final on aggregate, but the experience almost made up for the disappointment.

George Geddis was still my best pal and when we were both 13 we and several other mates wanted to join the Aberdeen Lads club, for whom my brother George played. There was no problem with us joining but they did not have a team for our age group, so we decided that the only thing to do was to create one and, with the club's approval, George and I enlisted help from the others and set about raising funds to buy kit and equipment. We were quite successful, in particular with a football lottery ticket which proved to be very popular in the city, and after a few weeks we had raised enough money to set up the side. Aberdeen Colts was born. Our fixtures were arranged for Saturday afternoons, which meant that we had very busy weekends. On Saturday mornings we played for the school and in the afternoons we played for Aberdeen Lads Colts. Sundays were spent kicking about to pass the time until we were back at school the next day. Bliss! (By the way, if this book falls into the hands of anyone currently playing for Aberdeen

Lads Colts, keep up the good work and remember how the side was founded in the early 1950s.)

I should point out something else that I hope may encourage any of today's youngsters who have the same problem that I endured all those years ago. There was an hereditary eye problem in our family and, as a result, one of my eyes used to live a life of its own. People said that I was cross-eyed because that is how it looked. It meant that I developed a squint from a very early age and had to wear glasses all the time from when I was about five.

My glasses were of the round-framed National Health sort and made me look a total nerd. I hated them but I had to wear them. I often came in for some stick from the other lads. That is the strange thing about kids – they can be the cruellest and yet at the same time the kindest people that you are ever likely to meet. The trouble was that I wore my glasses when I played football in the playground and in the street and as a result there were frequent breakages. Often for long periods I had no glasses at all and I had the choice of staying in all the time or subjecting myself to the taunts as my dodgy eye put on a show for everyone.

I did not wear my glasses for serious football matches. To anyone observing me, my method for combating my sight problem would have appeared hilarious. I used to keep my glasses on until the last possible moment. When the time came for us to go out on to the pitch I would take them off and close my right eye, which was the problem one. I would then play the entire game with one eye closed. My left eye was fine and, when it did not have to contend with the strange visions collected by my right eye, it served me very well.

Opponents and referees seeing me for the first time used to stare as I ran around with one eye closed. I was often asked if I had some dirt in my eye and I had to reassure everyone that this was not the case, without actually letting them in on my little secret. Some people even thought I was blind in one eye and looked at me with sympathy as if I had only one leg.

Others thought I was totally mad. I didn't mind the latter so much because at least it meant they gave me a wide berth in case my affliction was catching or I went completely off my rocker.

So that was the great Denis Law. Skinny, a dodgy eye, and wearing cast-off boots. I was not exactly a glamorous player in those days. But I was learning all the time and if there is one thing that any sort of handicap teaches you it is determination. I probably worked all the harder and was all the more strong-willed because I had an obstacle to overcome that the rest of my team-mates and opponents didn't. I was determined that they would have no grounds on which to taunt me about my sight, so I made sure that I played my heart out in every game.

At Christmas 1953, my mother gave me a very big leg-up in my football career. My mother did a great job in bringing up the family while my father was away, and managed to keep us in food and clothing on the low wage that he brought home. My father, who was a very proud man, realized this, but was totally opposed to us having any form of credit. On the quiet, my mother joined some credit schemes with two or three of the major stores in Aberdeen. She was not wasteful and would only use those schemes for what she considered to be essentials, and she always paid them promptly.

Without me dropping any hints at all, she knew that the best Christmas present she could possibly buy me would be a new pair of football boots. I was playing for the Aberdeen Lads Colts at the time and I think she recognized that I could not go on playing in second-hand boots for ever, even though I was quite prepared to if it meant playing rather than not playing. She also realized that I would know far better than she what boots to buy. That is why, on Christmas Eve, she handed me her credit card for Clydesdale's Store and told me to go and get myself some new boots. Anyone who was in Aberdeen on that day – and has a good memory! – may remember that it was snowing very heavily, but for me the sun was shining when I took the tram to the store and selected myself a pair of Hotspur boots.

Those boots meant everything to me. They would be museum pieces now because they were the real old-fashioned sort which came high up over the ankles and were heavy enough to keep a diver on the sea-bed for months. When I got them home, I spent several hours on that Christmas Eve with my feet in them soaking in a bowl of water to soften the leather. For all the time that I had those boots I looked after them as though they were the Crown Jewels. After every game they were carefully cleaned and dubbined to preserve them and make them sparkle for the next time that I wore them. They had to be kept hidden when my father was at home because the secret of my mother's credit card accounts might have been discovered. I don't think he ever knew.

Although I was playing a lot of football, I did not give up on my academic work. Had I not become a professional footballer, I might have done my best to fulfil my prospects as an architect, although in truth, in a bid to earn as quickly as possible, I would probably have taken any job as long as it did not mean going out to sea. I find it worrying when I hear that youngsters today are so convinced that they will make it as pros that they neglect their school work. I have seen various examples of how that can be a mistake. Young players have had everything going for them, only for their careers to be wrecked by injury. That sort of thing can happen to anyone, and it has to many, so don't be tempted to give up on your school work just because you happen to be half decent at football.

I have often heard discussions about how schoolboy internationals rarely go on to become stars of the game. In many cases they don't even become professionals. For me it worked out virtually the other way round. I was continuing to progress through the various years of schools' football and played for Aberdeen under-15s, thanks to my performances for the school team.

There were three other lads with that Aberdeen side who

later became professionals. For me the most memorable was Alex Dawson because we both later played for United, though not at the same time. But there were also John Ogston and Gordon Low, both of whom were achievers in the game.

As a result of being watched while with the Aberdeen Schools side, I was invited to join the Scotland Schoolboys squad for a game against Northern Ireland. You can imagine the excitement in the family when that invitation arrived. There was extra excitement for me too because the game was to be played away and I had never before ventured outside Scotland. It was to be my first trip 'abroad'.

If you look in the records you will not find my name on the list of Scotland schoolboy internationals because I never did play. I joined the squad and took an active part in the preparations but, when the great day arrived, I was not on the team sheet. There were no substitutes then, so whatever eleven were picked that was it for the game. I was on the bench to watch the match and gain the experience of being there, but I would dearly have loved to play. Being involved was an immense thrill but I was disappointed not to be able to pull on a Scotland shirt for the first time. I wish there had been substitutes then because I believe I would probably have been used for at least a short part of the game.

I returned home slightly embarrassed at not having played, but everyone else thought that it was honour enough to have been even considered and to have been there with the team. I was reassured that I would probably get my big chance next time. Nobody was aware that there would not be a next time. My schoolboy international career was over before it had begun because something was about to happen that would change my life for ever.

Just before Easter in 1955 there was a knock at our door. A man stood there and asked to speak to my parents about me. In my eyes that could mean only one thing – I was in trouble for something. When a stranger knocked at your door in those days and formally asked to have a chat, most people were already halfway out of the back window. Unfortunately there was no escape from our place so I had to stay and face whatever music was likely to be played.

The music turned out to be something very special. The man was Archie Beattie and we discovered that he was the brother of former Scotland international Andy Beattie, who was at that time the manager of Huddersfield Town. Archie was acting as scout for his brother and the reason for his call was to invite me for trials at the club. My mother was more than a little alarmed at the thought of her youngest son disappearing into the sunset for a while, but Archie assured her that he would not be sending me all the way down to Huddersfield unless he was confident that I had a very good chance of being offered a contract.

The timing could not have been better. The trials were due to take place during the Easter period and, since I was fast approaching the time when I would be leaving school, it could not have been a more opportune time. I would at least find out if I had a job to go to when I did leave school. It was also a tremendous thrill to know that Huddersfield were interested. Up to that moment I had never considered playing football as a future occupation, but now things were beginning to change in my mind. I did not think that Huddersfield would be very impressed when they saw me. I looked more like a drowned chicken than a would-be professional sportsman, but I determined to do my best to show what I could do.

My mother took a little persuading. Travelling to Northern Ireland with the Scotland Schoolboys was one thing, but staying in a foreign country like England for four or five weeks was something entirely different. When she discovered that my brothers John and George could travel with me, she warmed a little more to the idea but I think she was finally won over when she saw my face. I could hardly contain myself and, even though I was expecting to be back in Aberdeen fairly soon, I really wanted to go.

When she finally agreed I could have given her the biggest

hug of her life. Once again my mother had come up trumps when it was really needed. My squint and I were bound for Huddersfield.

2

YES, MR SHANKLY

It was a very strange feeling to be going over the border into England, knowing that I was embarking upon a journey that might just mean that I would not be coming back in a hurry. My own thoughts were that Huddersfield would politely tell me that it had been a nice idea but that was as far as it went. Archie Beattie's encouraging words, though, had meant that there was just a chance that I might indeed be staying at Huddersfield for a while. John, George and I pressed our faces close to the window as we saw Scotland disappear behind us, and England took us into her bosom.

When our train pulled into Huddersfield station I looked around for someone from the club. At first I couldn't see anyone. My brothers were also scanning the few people at the railway station. Then I saw a man looking at me. He was staring with an expression of disbelief and mild horror at this skinny little lad with National Health glasses, a bag in one hand and a train ticket in the other. A lad who looked, and was, a fish out of water.

The man was Eddie Brennan, one of the Huddersfield administrators. He was very kind, but I could tell that he thought there must have been some mistake. First of all we were taken to the club and afterwards to meet my landlady, Mrs Clark, who ran a boarding place called Pond House. Several young players were staying there and it was also used by show business people performing in the area. I don't think Eddie Brennan could wait to leave us to go and find out what exactly had gone wrong.

My brothers were able to stay for a day or two and that was a big help to me, especially since the very next day after my arrival I was due to take part in a practice match. I knew that everyone would be looking at me and expecting me to fail. It served only to make me all the more determined to let them know that I was, at least, not totally useless. As it happened, I had a good game and people began to talk to me rather differently.

After a couple of days my brothers had to return to Scotland. I went with them to the railway station and waved them off. As I watched their train glide out I almost wanted to run after them. I felt dreadful. I was already lonely, in a foreign country without a friend in sight. It was homesickness with a vengeance.

My trial continued and as each day went by I became more and more aware that I was missing my family and friends. Huddersfield, however, seemed to be no nearer to packing me off home. At last I was summoned to the office and prepared myself to hear all the reasons why they were sending me back. I just wanted to get it over with and get on the next available train. Consequently I was extremely surprised when they offered me a contract on amateur terms. I would receive five pounds a week but, like all the other ground-staff lads, I would have to work hard at painting, cleaning, looking after kit, cleaning boots, making tea and performing all the other menial tasks that seemed to be everlastingly available. Homesickness or not, I accepted of course.

Andy Beattie was manager of Huddersfield and, when Bill Shankly arrived, he took over the running of the reserves. I was a youth team player and therefore saw little of them except when they came to watch now and then. Because of that, it came as more of a surprise when Andy Beattie noticed that I was not getting over my homesickness. We chatted about

15

things in general and he asked about my eyes. I told him that we had already applied for me to have an operation to put my lazy eye to work properly and that I was waiting to hear. He also asked if I had any pals back in Aberdeen who were good at football and might be useful to the club. I mentioned Gordon Low and, within a short space of time, Gordon had joined us at Huddersfield. It was the start of a career which saw him play something like 400 senior games in England.

My homesickness slowly evaporated when Gordon came to the club. I also received the good news that my operation appointment had come through, and life began to look a little rosier. We worked hard and our spare time was mostly spent at the digs listening to records or playing cards. Occasionally we went to the cinema or to a local snooker hall but, in general, we were encouraged to go to bed early and, though I say it myself, we were quite well behaved. In addition to our work with Huddersfield we were also encouraged to keep an eye on the future, just in case our prospective football careers came to nothing. I continued my interest in technical drawing at a local institute and Gordon and I also found work with a local paint-ing firm for a day and a half every week. We didn't enjoy it very much because we were given the filthiest jobs and most of our evening was spent trying to peel, wash, or rasp some very determined paint from our skin.

At long last the date for my operation arrived and I travelled back to Aberdeen. I was operated on by a woman. She was very skilled and took a great deal of pride in her work. Then the big moment came for the bandages to be removed and she told me to go and have a look for myself in the mirror. What I saw frightened the life out of me. My eye was bloodshot and bruised and I looked just as if I had been beaten to a pulp by a heavyweight boxer. Then, all at once, I realized that I could actually see myself properly. My eye remained where it should and did not go wandering off to look at something else. I was ecstatic! It was a very emotional moment and I could not stop saying thank you to the lady who had performed this miracle.

She told me that the best way I could thank her would be to go and make something of my career. I really hope that she was pleased with the result.

With my eyes now in unison, my life changed dramatically. I no longer had any need to wear glasses. I no longer had to close one eye when I was playing football. I no longer had to look away when people were talking to me. Unless you have actually experienced something like that it is very difficult to explain how it feels. I can only say that I shed tears of gratitude.

Although my sight was now pretty good, it was far from perfect and I have always suffered slightly blurred vision in my right eye. Throughout my career, and up to this day, I have never had perfect vision. I did not shout about it because I did not want anyone to know. Perhaps, if it had been common knowledge, one or two managers who signed me might have had second thoughts. It is very hard to convince someone that you can see even though your vision is blurred, and misunderstandings might well have resulted. I thought it best to let everyone think that I could see as clearly as them. Fortunately my left eye never let me down and so I got away with it.

I made progress in the youth team, as did Gordon Low. We were both selected to play for the Northern Intermediate League side which was quite an honour. We also enjoyed some great games against the youth teams of other League sides including that of Manchester United, whose side contained quite a few of the boys who were to become the Busby Babes. I nearly became one myself at that time, I believe.

Although we lost 2–4 to the United side, I had quite a good match and I was told that Matt Busby had made a note of me. I later learned that Huddersfield were offered a fee for me more than once. Matt Busby had offered £10,000, which was a lot of money for a lad who had only just turned 16.

There were other bids for me too, and I'm told that West Bromwich Albion was among them. I did not know too much about all this at the time of course. I was just happy to be

17

playing football for Huddersfield's youth side. I was a little less happy when the first team was relegated from the First Division at the end of the 1955–56 season – although, for me, it turned out to be a blessing in disguise.

As the first team struggled that season it became obvious that some of the Huddersfield senior players were now past their best. As a result there were constant changes between the first team and the reserves, which often left gaps in the reserves side. I was called up for them and found myself under the direction of Bill Shankly.

Shankly made a big difference to me because he was always so positive and enthusiastic about his team and his players. He helped me a lot, not least because he was keen that I should build up my strength. To that end he put me on a diet which involved a lot of steak and milk. Since I had only rarely eaten meat as a boy, an unlimited amount of steak was just incredible and I did not object in the slightest. On the down side, however, Shanks also made me drink China tea without milk or sugar. It was revolting!

On Christmas Eve 1956, just a few short years after my mother had given me a new pair of football boots for Christmas, I had another great Christmas present. I was told that I would be travelling with the first team to Meadow Lane as part of the squad for the game against Notts County. I did not know whether I would actually be playing until after I got there, so imagine my excitement and delight when I was told to go and get changed.

The Meadow Lane pitch was very muddy, but to me it was paradise as I ran out wearing the No. 8 shirt for my first ever senior game. I was 16 years and 10 months old and I was still an amateur but here I was, playing for Huddersfield's first team. It was amazing. On the right wing was Kevin McHale, and he was only four months older than me, so between us we formed one of the youngest partnerships the game has ever seen. The icing on the cake came with the final whistle as we won 2–1. Two days later, on Boxing Day, we played the return game, and this time we won 3–0. I am proud to say that I scored one of our goals, my first in senior football. What a Christmas that was.

The following month Andy Beattie surprised everyone by deciding to retire. Andy had been very kind to me and given me my big chance in the game and I knew we would miss him. He was a quiet man, a complete contrast to the man who now took over as No. 1 at Huddersfield, Bill Shankly.

There has never been anyone quite like Shankly. He was his own man and did everything in his own way. I got on well with him. I had established myself in the first team and I was one of Shanks' players from the reserves. He was one of the most passionate men that I have ever known and expected his players to give everything every time they changed into their kit. It did not matter if you were just playing in a five-a-side game in training, you still had to show the hunger that Shankly himself always felt. He was a great manager and I enjoyed being one of his players. His team-talks were something else. He would tear apart the opposition both as a team and individually. Had they heard him and taken him at his word, I think many of them would have retired from the game.

Shankly talked up everything and everyone with whom he was involved. His own players were the best in the universe and his team could fly to the moon and back without transport. If you were injured, though, he would ignore you. That took a bit of getting used to. There you were, expecting some sympathy, and all you got was the cold shoulder to add to your other ailments. The corridors at Huddersfield's old Leeds Road ground were quite narrow and it was impossible to walk past someone without seeing them. Shankly had it off to a fine art, though. If you came out of the treatment room as he was walking towards you, he would start whistling and look at the ceiling until you were past him and out of sight. He literally pretended that you were not there. It wasn't just me. I have talked to many other players, both

19

at Huddersfield and Liverpool, and they have all said the same thing.

If you happened to mention the word 'defeat' to Bill Shankly, he would have to look it up in the dictionary. It was a word that had no place in his vocabulary. He hated losing – totally detested it. I sometimes think that he would have preferred burglars to ransack his house than to lose a football match.

In spite of all those foibles, he was a terrific man and very understanding of what it was like for a young lad living away from home, trying to carve out a career in football. He had been through it himself when he was in his teens, and he often demonstrated that he knew what life was like for us. I can remember our landlady once phoning him and telling him to get over to our digs right away because there was some trouble. I had punched one of the other lads, Billy McDonald, because he had been insulting. Poor old Billy had quite a black eye by the time Shanks appeared. Gordon Low explained what had happened and Shankly turned round to Billy and told him to be more careful about what he said in future.

I used to be a bit hot-headed in those days and I know that I must quite often have been a pain in the backside to Bill Shankly and his assistants. I would challenge them to football matches in the car park when most of the others had gone home and, if they refused, I used to goad them into playing. Since I was a lot younger than them, I wore them out. It backfired on me, though, because I ended up with a strangely swollen leg which put me in hospital for a while. It was diagnosed as over-work and I had my wings clipped so that I did not train or play any more than was appropriate for a lad of my age.

After my 17th birthday in February 1957, I was free to sign for any club I chose because I was only an amateur and therefore Huddersfield had no legal hold on me. A number of clubs were interested, among them Rangers and Celtic. I think the newspapers did what they still do today and listed just about every major club on the planet as having an interest in me.

My father travelled down from Aberdeen to discuss the matter and we had a great weekend together. We played Peterborough in the FA Cup on the Saturday and won 3–1. I scored our first goal. My dad went back to Aberdeen on the Sunday evening and, just before he went, I signed professional forms for Huddersfield. It was tempting to go elsewhere but Shankly was a very persuasive man and by the time he had pleaded Huddersfield's case, I think both my dad and myself would have felt really bad if I had not signed. When I went to bed that night I kept having to remind myself that I was now a professional footballer. I half-expected to wake up the following morning to discover that I had been dreaming.

We reached the fifth round of the FA Cup that season and I was disappointed when we lost 1–2 to Burnley. There was no real need for shame because Burnley were a very strong First Division side, but signing as a professional had made me even more hungry for success. I was well aware that a footballer's career has a limited number of years, and that most players end their careers just as most people are beginning theirs. I wanted to be successful and make the most of my time.

Bill Shankly continued to be a big influence on my game. As my manager he helped me to develop my abilities. He had a simple approach and encouraged us to 'work on your weaknesses and let your strengths take care of themselves'. I often hear television commentators today talking about a player missing the target because he had the ball 'on his weaker left foot'. That would have definitely cut no ice with Bill Shankly. He believed that you should not have a weakness in your game and, if you did, he expected you to work like mad to get rid of it. He was right too. We were professionals, picked because of our abilities, and expected to deliver in return for our wages. If a plumber said, 'I'm all right on U-bends but I'm not very good on taps', you'd send for another plumber. It's just the same with professional footballers.

Under Shankly's control, Huddersfield put a stop to the downward spiral and we began to get our act together. There

21

was, of course, that memorable occasion when we played at Charlton and went from being 5–1 ahead with twenty minutes left, to losing 6–7. Shankly went absolutely crazy. I didn't like the idea of Huddersfield losing, but it didn't affect me too much as I was out of action and had to watch the game from the stands.

We finished the season in 12th place in the old Second Division. Just to give you some idea of what the competition was like then, Leicester were top of the division with Nottingham Forest in second place, Liverpool third, and Blackburn Rovers fourth. Only the top two were promoted. Manchester United were League Champions.

We were quite revved up for the following season which began in August 1957. Shankly had us believing in ourselves and we were ready to take on anyone. The trouble was that there was no money available to strengthen the squad. A few seasons earlier, attendances at Leeds Road had been tremendous but, with the club dropping out of the top division and then struggling for a while before rallying in the Second Division, support had declined. All clubs in those days were very dependent upon attendance figures; there were no colossal television pay-outs. We needed more depth to the squad if we were to mount a serious challenge for promotion, but there was no cash available.

We still finished several places higher than the previous season and I had a very good season. Once again there had been talk of me moving to another club, but I had long since learned to take all that with a pinch of salt. If there is nothing much happening in the news, then speculation begins to take over.

The biggest news of that season came in February 1958, and had nothing to do with my birthday. We had finished training and I was hanging around at the ground when word came through that the plane carrying Manchester United home from a European match had crashed at Munich. Bill Shankly was visibly shaken when he heard the news. He had the greatest respect for

Matt Busby and the first newsflashes reported that Matt had been killed along with quite a few of the players. We were all devastated. There was not much relief when we finally heard that Matt had survived because the shock of the event was so great.

I could not get it out of my head and I certainly did not sleep that night. In my limited time in England I had seen most of those players and even played against some of them. The thought that they were dead just wouldn't sink in. It was some days later, when I was still thinking about it, that I realized that, if Huddersfield had accepted that offer of £10,000 from Manchester United, I might well have been one of the players on that plane. It was a sobering thought and one that I have never fully banished from my mind. (It is history now that Matt Busby eventually recovered, and that he and I were to share some great moments in the future.)

During the summer of 1958 all eyes were turned towards Sweden where the World Cup was to be held. All four of the home nations qualified, but only Wales and Northern Ireland went further than the group stages. I looked on and wondered if I might play for Scotland one day. I had to remind myself to be realistic. After all, I was playing for Huddersfield in the English Second Division, not exactly in the sort of spotlight from which international selectors pick their men.

The star of that summer, and probably the star of the game ever since, was Pelé, the youngest World Cup winner of all time. He had made his senior international début only the year before and he certainly stole the show in Sweden as Brazil stormed to victory. I looked on, slightly enviously, especially when I learned that Pelé was eight months younger than me.

My own record was just around the corner, although I did not know it, as we started the 1958–59 season. Everyone had been talking about the Brazilians, but when the English season began, it was back to the bread and butter of League football. We started well enough and I found myself scoring a few goals, but the competition was very strong and I think we knew that

23

we would be battling to stay in the division rather than heading for a promotion place.

In October 1958 my world changed dramatically. I was staggered to be called into the Scotland squad by Matt Busby, who by then had not only recovered from Munich but had taken charge of Scotland, in addition to his role as manager of Manchester United. The drinks flowed in Aberdeen once I told the family, and there were a lot of proud people gathered round the radio when I made my début for the Scottish senior side in a 3–0 win over Wales in Cardiff. At the end of the game my name was on the scoresheet – it was the start of my international career.

The word 'thrill' has been used so often that it has become totally inadequate to describe how I felt about making my Scotland début. I never expected such a bonus. Bill Shankly was thrilled for me too. He had played for Scotland in his day, but the best years of his playing career had been occupied by the Second World War, so he enjoyed just a taste of what might have been. He helped me to keep my feet on the ground and reminded me that I still had a lot of work to do if I was going to be a decent player. That was the amazing thing about Shankly. He made you feel you could walk on water one minute, and like a total novice the next. Either way you were putty in his hands and just felt the way he wanted you to feel about yourself.

Ray Wilson was one of my team-mates at Huddersfield and a better defender it would be hard to find. He was quick, tough and very difficult to play against in training. He later joined Everton and then became one of that exclusive band of people who have won the World Cup. I prefer to think of him as a team-mate at Huddersfield where we grew up together. He was always being linked with potential transfers and it became something of a joke – until it finally happened.

Ray had made his first-team début shortly before I made mine and he had been in the army before he joined Huddersfield, so he had been around a little more than I had.

We were good pals off the pitch, but if we were ever on opposing sides in training, then there were some fireworks. I would do my best to run him ragged and he tried hard to shake my confidence – and my teeth, my legs, and anything else that would vibrate after one of his tackles. He was such a good player that I could forgive him for being English – almost!

Having been reminded by Shankly that my bread and butter came before my international career, I got on with the job of scoring goals for Huddersfield. It had become harder, though. I played with a bit of a swagger and always had something to say for myself – so I was an immediate target for the abuse of opposition supporters. Now that I had been capped by Scotland amid so much publicity because of my age, I was most definitely a marked man. Opposing players, urged on by their fans, were no longer prepared to give me the benefit of any doubt. Every tackle was meant to intimidate, rile and generally put me off my game, either mentally or physically. I had to find new strengths of character to combat this and to show that I would not be intimidated. The result was that I swaggered and showed off even more and generally made myself increasingly unpopular among those who did not support Huddersfield Town. They were the majority, of course.

One of the results of this change of attitude was that I put much more into my own tackles and gradually began to earn a reputation for being something of a rough player. Yes, that bespectacled weakling who had joined Huddersfield just a few years earlier was getting a reputation for being one of the game's most fiery and toughest customers. What is so silly is that it was completely out of character. I have never been the sort to allow other people to run all over me, but I have never gone looking for trouble either. Mind you, some people don't have to go looking for trouble, they automatically attract it. I'm one of them.

As 1958 was about to close, I twisted my knee playing against Charlton. I thought it would be all right but when it still hurt during the next game it became obvious that I had done some real damage. The problem turned out to be a cartilage torn in three places and the only cure for that was a spell in hospital. I missed the next couple of months of the season, but I was back before it ended.

By the end of that season it was plain to see that Bill Shankly's long-term plan was beginning to be realized. We finished in 14th place, but there were only three points between the team which finished eighth – Charlton – and Ipswich, who finished in 16th position. Having no money to spend encouraged Bill Shankly to put more emphasis on his youth development programme and now those youngsters were beginning to come through. Our young team could have fared a lot worse. We had not gone beyond the third round of the FA Cup, where we had been knocked out by Ipswich, but at least we had not been dumped out by non-League opposition, which had been the fate of Liverpool.

The mention of Liverpool is quite deliberate. The 1959–60 season was just a few months old, and we were playing really well, when Bill Shankly left to become manager at Anfield. It was a blow because we really thought that this was going to be our promotion year. We had certainly started well enough. At the end of the season Huddersfield occupied sixth place.

The transfer speculation had built up again during the early part of the season and clubs such as Rangers, Chelsea, Everton and Arsenal were said to be interested. To his credit, Bill Shankly kept me informed of the true situation and there were, apparently, some genuine enquiries. Everton had bid £40,000 for me and had been turned down. The newspapers were going on about me being the subject of a British record transfer and it was suggested that, since I had been in the game for only five minutes, such a deal would be ridiculous. I found that I was being used for target practice when, really, any such transfer speculation was nothing to do with me.

I was still at Huddersfield in December when Bill Shankly went to Liverpool – though I was to leave not long after. Eddie Boot took over as manager. Eddie was a nice man and had been of great assistance to Shankly, but he was a totally different sort of character. We had become accustomed to the rough, gruff approach of Shanks, and it was quite a culture shock to be managed by Eddie Boot who was so amazingly quiet. It was a bit like going into a library after being out on a busy street filled with traffic.

One of Eddie's first jobs during his early weeks in charge was to call me into the club one evening for what I knew was to be a transfer discussion. It had been reported that I did not want to go to a London club because it would be even further from Scotland. That was not true. Actually, I quite fancied going to Arsenal and, as I travelled down to Leeds Road on that evening in March 1960, I fully expected to be meeting the then Highbury boss, George Swindin. (Today's youngsters turn up for such a meeting in an Aston Martin, a Ferrari, or are chauffeur-driven. I went on a trolley-bus.)

I was disappointed to find that the Arsenal manager was not there. It made me think twice about Arsenal. If they were not bothered about talking to me, then I would return their lack of interest. I had half-expected that Liverpool would make a bid for me but later discovered that Bill Shankly could not do so as he had no money available. It had been Shankly who had turned down the bid from Everton and he did not feel that Huddersfield would accept a much lower bid from himself at Liverpool, as he later explained to me.

Manchester United had shown no interest at all, which quite surprised me because Matt Busby had been very kind to me when I had played for Scotland and I knew about the bid he had made for me several years earlier. Again it was later explained to me by Matt that he did not bid for me simply because he did not need me at that time. He already had enough talent for his purposes and he was not the sort of manager who would buy just for the sake of it, or to stop a player going to a rival club.

When I arrived at Leeds Road that evening it was Les McDowall, manager of Manchester City, who was introduced to me. I had never even thought of going to Maine Road, yet they were a very big club and considered to be among the élite of the First Division. The more Les McDowall talked, the more I began to fancy the idea. I had pangs about leaving Huddersfield, but I knew that it was bound to happen sooner or later, so I listened intently and finally agreed to move.

The two clubs settled on a transfer fee of £55,000, which was indeed a new British record. In those days the transfer scene was very different from that of today and I was not entitled to any share of the agreed amount, or a signing-on fee of any sort. Eddie Boot told me that I would receive a gift of £300.

To be absolutely honest – I'm still waiting for it.

3

SEVEN GOALS, AND WE LOST

The glamour and fireworks of the First Division had lured me to Manchester City, but by the time I had been at Maine Road for just a few weeks, I realized that some of the sequins had fallen off and that there were more than a few damp squibs among the rockets, bangers and catherine wheels. Manchester City was not all that I had expected it to be.

I had been dazzled by their image. They were a big club with many successes to their credit and a great reputation. For many years they had been the rich neighbours of Manchester United. It is a funny thing in football, but clubs which have had a good spell often retain the image of a major player for decades afterwards, even if they should slide down to the bottom of the division.

Not that I'm suggesting that Manchester City had fallen from grace but, when I signed, I was under the impression that their position near the foot of the First Division was simply the result of a temporary loss of form. I was also under the impression that moving to a club like City would be a big step up from Huddersfield Town. You can imagine then what a culture shock it was when I pulled on the famous Manchester City training kit for the first time, only to find that the shirt was frayed and even had a few holes in it.

I thought that someone was playing a dressing-room joke on me – that is, until I looked at my team-mates and realized that

29

their shirts were as badly worn as mine and, in some cases, even worse. That city gear spoke volumes. I was amazed. This was not at all what I had been expecting. The Leeds Road ground may not have been as big as Maine Road, and Huddersfield Town were in the next division down from City, but our kit and our facilities had been in tip-top condition and we had always been proud to wear the shirt. Those City shirts spoke volumes about the club's lowly position in the First Division. The club was in a winter of discontent in which bad attitudes prevailed, and there was a famine of pride. Very quickly I became as disenchanted as everyone else.

There were of course some very good players in the team. Bert Trautmann was in goal, and I have seen none better. He was still in good form when I joined Manchester City and I dread to think how badly the side might have fared had he also been off colour. Alan Oakes was in the team as well. He was a young inexperienced lad at that time but was obviously destined for better days ahead. The trouble with City, apart from the attitude problem, was that they had become far too dependent upon players of yesterday. I'm not saying that they were bad players; in fact some of them had been great. However, for the most part, they were past their best. One or two youngsters were included, but the general idea seemed to be to have one player as a 'star', and all the others seemed to be either on their way out or had not actually arrived yet.

If you add that combination to an existing bad club attitude, and a board that seemed determined not to speculate, you have a very unhealthy environment and a football club that is hovering perilously close to the trap-door of doom. Sadly, City have been going through another bad patch in recent years, but hopefully this is just a phase from which the club will bounce back.

When I joined in March 1960, the fight was on to avoid relegation from what was then the top division. My first game was away to Leeds and I scored one of our three goals. No celebrations, though, because Leeds scored four. It was a little ironic that, at the end of the season, Leeds were relegated while we managed to scrape clear. However, it was a very tight relegation fight with only seven points between the bottom eight clubs.

The summer of 1960 was something of a respite yet, when we reported back for pre-season training, it seemed almost as if we had never had a close season at all. It did not help when I made no secret of the fact that I disliked the training methods being employed.

I had enjoyed the Shankly approach, which meant a lot of ball work and five-a-sides. At Manchester City there was a preoccupation with our physical development and I seemed to spend all my training time running around the ground or up and down the terraces. Some days I never even saw a football at all. I used to argue with our trainer, Jimmy Meadows. I once suggested that it might be a better idea if we were entered for the Grand National as our training programme was better suited to running and jumping our way around Aintree than it was to playing a game of football. My many objections caused me to be hauled up in front of our manager, Les McDowall, on more than one occasion. Les used to make a show of siding with Jimmy but it never went any further because the boss did not want to upset me. I am sure that deep down inside he was in full agreement with me, but he did not want to upset Jimmy Meadows either.

As you can see, I was not easy to live with. I am the first to admit that fact. I had already earned a reputation for being extremely quick to flare up and quite often happy to enter into a punch-up at the drop of a hat. A lot of people referred to me as big-headed. The truth of the matter was that, while I was arrogant, I was soon ready to back down if I discovered that I was in the wrong. On the subject of training I knew I was right. At Huddersfield I had worked with one of the very best and I did not appreciate joining a supposedly bigger club only to be forced into lowering my performance standards.

The 1960–61 season was a joke. We had no consistency at all and, in hindsight, I have to say that it was because we had no confidence as a team. We were disjointed and while certain individuals were often playing well, we did not perform as a unit. The buck has to stop at management level for that. The first half of the season was a nightmare and by Christmas we were struggling to avoid the dreaded drop once again. To add insult to injury we were also out of the new League Cup competition, having been beaten by Portsmouth, who should have been fairly easy prey for us.

There was only the slightest of improvements in the New Year. Our big problem was that we were bad when we played away. Our worst defeats were always away from home. Our home record was not too bad but we could not seem to do anything right when we played away. We leaked far too many goals. In 21 games away from home we conceded 60 goals, which is a poor record. When we played away to Cardiff in the FA Cup we struggled – even though they were battling against relegation in the division below us.

If one of the Cardiff players had not scored an own goal on that cold January day, a little piece of football would never have happened. As it was, we came away from Cardiff grateful for a 1–1 draw. The replay at Maine Road should have been a formality but, in the end, we drew 0–0 and had to play again, this time on the neutral ground of Highbury. At the end of 90 minutes it was still 0–0 but in extra time Joe Hayes and I scored a goal each and we were through to the next round of the competition at last. We were a very relieved side when we heard that final whistle, I can tell you.

The fourth round tie was against Luton, a fellow First Division side, who were then being managed by the former legendary Charlton goalkeeper, Sam Bartram. The game was to be played at Kenilworth Road and when we saw the state of the pitch we wondered that we had been told to turn up at all. We changed slowly, expecting at any minute to hear that the match had been postponed. There was no such cancellation, however, and so we squelched our way on to the pitch and warmed up by trying to perform *Swan Lake* on a surface that partly resembled a paddy-field with the rest like a giant patch of really thick, cold, off-colour porridge.

Luton had the reputation for starting a game like grey-hounds, but we did not expect them to start as anything more than wallowing hippos on that pitch. We were totally wrong. In just over a quarter of an hour they scored twice. I was annoyed. I could not believe that we had travelled all the way from Manchester to play on a bog, and then get hammered into the bargain. My annoyance reflected in my play. I did not start kicking people but I stepped up a gear and found that, by running on my toes even more, I could stop myself from getting stuck in the mud. The Luton defenders remained flat-footed and, within a minute of the second home goal, I pulled one back.

I suddenly became aware that, while everyone else seemed to be slipping and sliding, I was able to keep my feet, turn easily and sprint. By half-time I had headed home two more goals, and from being two goals down we sloshed our way back into the dressing room with a 3–2 lead. In the second half we just carried on from where we had left off and I could not stop scoring. In just over 20 minutes of the second half I scored another three and we were pretty confident that we would be in the draw for the next round.

We were still celebrating the sixth goal when we realized that the referee was taking another look at the state of the pitch. If it had been bad at the start it now looked as if a dozen elephants had been rolling about in it. The rain was beating down even harder and, with 21 minutes of the game left to play, the ref decided that enough was enough. Luton were delighted of course. Manchester City were stunned and I was in a state of total disbelief.

To his credit, our boss Les McDowall did protest. His argument was that, since the game had gone as far as it had, it was ridiculous not to complete it. I think he had a point, but then I would, wouldn't I? His Luton opposite number, Sam Bartram, could not stop chuckling. It was a good-natured chuckle and anyone else finding themselves in the same position would have been equally amused and delighted. I think I would have been hysterical.

That, of course, was not the end of the story. The game had to be played again at Kenilworth Road and this time it would be a mid-week affair. Someone at our club did not like the look of their floodlights and so it was agreed to have an afternoon kick-off. We fielded the same side but Luton made quite a few alterations. They made no change to their swashbuckling style, however, and roared right into the game once the referee had blown his whistle. Such was their charge that, if he had been in the way, I think the referee would have been trampled underfoot.

After just over 20 minutes we were two goals adrift once again. I think the City fans were half-expecting me to slip into a telephone box and change into SuperLaw. I did my best but Luton had adopted different tactics. Instead of trying to mark me out of the game, they just stifled the service, so I saw much less of the ball than I had in the previous game. I managed to pull a goal back before half-time but, with the scene all set for a repeat performance of the onslaught of several days earlier, it was Luton who scored the next goal. My pal, Ken Barnes, had been injured and was reduced to nuisance value on the wing, which meant that we virtually had only ten men – and a hill to climb. We did not climb it.

I can laugh about it now but at the time the events of the FA Cup fourth round only served to make me even more frustrated at my lot in life. Now that the two cup possibilities were out of reach we had to concentrate on staying in the First Division. We did improve a little and finished two places higher than in the previous season, although with exactly the same number of points.

Looking back on that season, there were a number of notable things both good and bad. The bad ones included losing both derby games against Manchester United. I had never played in derby games before and I had heard all sorts of tales about how tough they were, how different they were, and how much was at stake. I had scoffed at these stories. To me, a football match was simply a football match. It did not matter who you were playing – it was all the same. After losing twice to Manchester United I changed my mind. All that I had heard about derby games was true. I never enjoyed them one little bit – even those we won. They are a distraction, like a cup tie. You get caught up in the fever and cannot play your usual game.

A bonus that season was being selected to play for the Football League. In my first match for them we played against Northern Ireland, but it was my second game, against the Italian League, that was to prove such an important one for me.

On the down side I had a fall-out with Les McDowall in the latter days of the season. I was selected for Scotland but City wanted me for their crucial League matches. I wanted to play for Scotland and virtually said that I was going to – with or without permission. After a battle, permission was finally given. On the same day that Scotland suffered a heavy defeat, City drew 1–1 against West Ham.

I had unintentionally made no secret of the fact that if City were relegated I wanted to leave. I did not want my career to take a dive down a division, but I had kept my thoughts about that to myself until I was pushed on the subject by a newspaper reporter. I had learned the folly of talking to the press but I slipped up on this occasion and my innermost thoughts were plastered all over the sports pages. The club and some of its supporters did not like my honesty and I found myself being called all sorts of names. I can understand that from their point of view I must have appeared like a rodent leaving the *Titanic*, but few seemed to want to see it from where I was standing. Manchester City would still be there long after Denis Law had started collecting his pension. I had to do what was right for myself.

I have probably painted a dreadful picture of my time at Manchester City. There were, of course, some days when it was indeed dreadful and I was bitterly disappointed. I had not expected that moving to Maine Road would be such a step back from the progress I had been making at Huddersfield. However, there were many good days too, a lot of laughs and good friendships. My best pal was Ken Barnes, whose son Peter also played for Manchester City a decade later and was an apprentice when I returned to Maine Road.

With City having ensured safety, it seemed that I might be staying with the club after all, but I really did want to leave by this time. I could not see anything but another struggle the following season and I anticipated that it would go on like that until the club did finally suffer the drop. That was not the sort of experience or career I was seeking.

I began to wonder if someone else might be interested in me, but I could not think of any of the top clubs who had a need for a player like me. However, there had recently been a new development in football: British players were being recruited by the wealthy Italians. John Charles had already been a success in Italy for several years with Juventus, and it seemed that now the floodgates were about to open.

But was it likely? Denis Law in Italy? Denis Law, the weedy kid from Aberdeen?

In March 1961, when I had played for the Football League against the Italian League, it had simply never occurred to me that not only fans but club managers and chairmen were also watching keenly. Italy had beaten us 4–2, but it had been an exciting game and the newspapers were full of praise for both sides.

When I played for Scotland in April and we suffered that famous 9–3 defeat, among the crowd was a gentleman by the name of Gigi Peronace, who was looking for players for Italian clubs. I did not think there was much chance of him being interested in any of us after we lost so badly. The word on the street was that he was chiefly interested in Jimmy Greaves, but no doubt he had an open mind.

Nothing happened for two weeks, but then I received a telephone call from someone who said that he was in Britain on behalf of Helenio Herrera, the famous Italian coach who was in charge of Inter Milan. We met and, after some discussion, I realized just how big a financial gap there was between Italian and British football. I had been earning a basic £20 per week at City. The offer to go to Inter was more than twice that and included a signing fee of £5,000 and bonuses that amounted to £200 for a victory and £100 for a draw. It was like being offered the chance to win the lottery. By today's standards it is peanuts, but for me in 1961 the money in Italian football seemed amazing.

A few days after our initial meeting the man turned up again and this time he brought a draft contract. I was happy to sig it even though, as yet, there had been no contact between the two clubs and I had mentioned nothing of all this to Manchester City. It was probably wrong of me, but the contract was not binding if either of the two clubs did not agree, so I could not see any harm in signing and I enjoyed the cloak and dagger approach to my transfer.

It was only a few days after I had signed that Gigi Peronace suddenly turned up. He had already succeeded in signing Joe Baker from Hibernian for Torino and now he was on my case. I knew Joe Baker and was greatly interested in the possibility of going to an Italian club where I would, at least, share the experience with someone else from Britain. I was offered virtually the same deal as the one that had been suggested by the Inter representative, so I agreed. Now it was down to the two clubs.

City made it quite clear that they did not want me to leave. The chairman, Alan Douglas, offered me a huge pay rise which would have taken my weekly income to around £80. By British standards it was a great offer, but it just did not match up to Italian standards. Anyway, the reason I wanted to leave City was because the club seemed to be going nowhere but towards relegation within the next year or two.

I have to say that the chairman did go to great lengths to warn me that I would not be able to settle in Italy. He explained that it was not just the money that was different; the whole way of life would be a culture shock. I did not listen to him because I thought he was just resorting to saying anything to keep me at Maine Road. On reflection he was right in nearly everything he said.

My mind was made up that I wanted to go to Italy, and in particular to Torino. The two clubs, with Gigi Peronace negotiating, agreed a transfer fee of £110,000. It was a record at that time by an Italian club for a British player, so City had some compensation in that they had received double the money they had paid out for me when I joined from Huddersfield.

I was at Maine Road for about 15 months and during that time I played in 44 League matches and scored 21 goals. I also played in two League Cup games and in the FA Cup. I had scored twice in each of four games. But probably the game I remember best was the one City played on the Luton swamp and the six that got away.

I still have a great fondness for Manchester City. They are a very big club who have made their mark on the British game. They deserved better during my early days there and deserve better now. Their supporters are excellent, and with a following like that no club will stay in the doldrums for long. I look forward to seeing them back in the Premiership and the return of the derby days with United.

4

SCOTLAND FOR EVER

While I am sitting in the departure lounge awaiting the flight that will take me to Italy, I think that it might be a good time to reflect on playing for Scotland. Anyone who has ever represented their country at any sport will tell you that it is the single greatest honour that any sportsman can receive. Winning medals and trophies is, of course, wonderful – but being asked to wear the badge of your country is even more special.

It was always a big ambition of mine to play for Scotland in the World Cup finals. I had dreamed about it since I was a boy although I never really expected that one day it might actually happen. The Scotland side has been dogged for decades by odd results and many disappointments – with some spectacular successes mixed in. The Tartan Army has been regularly drained emotionally and yet it keeps coming back for more. It is still every Scottish schoolboy's dream to be able to play for his country.

It was Matt Busby, of all people, who gave me my first chance for Scotland. Quite incredibly Matt had recovered sufficiently from the horrendous crash in Munich in February 1958 not only to restore himself as manager of Manchester United, but also to take charge of Scotland. His style of management never failed to raise eyebrows and, when he selected his first Scotland team – to face Wales in October 1958 – he certainly put the cat among the pigeons. Many pundits of Scottish football were openly shocked when Matt picked a forward line of what were often labelled, quite wrongly as it happens, Anglo-Scots. I have never liked being called an Anglo-Scot. It suggests that I am some sort of a mongrel. I was born in Scotland, of Scottish parents, and I don't think you can get much more Scottish than that.

There were, and still are, some media people who seem to think that you can only be truly Scottish if you never set foot outside the old country. Actually, I'm not sure whether they really think that or if it is just an habitual part of writing their copy – like their never-ending preoccupation with ages. Whenever you read a newspaper report it is always well salted with ages. John Smith, aged 18, and Tom Smith, aged 24, were in court for stealing from Fred Jones, a 34-year-old milkman. The 64-year-old judge said . . . etc., etc. Who cares how old these people are? That same mentality causes every footballer whose work takes them across the Scottish border to be branded as an 'Anglo-Scot'. How ridiculous that sort of statement is.

As if it weren't bad enough that Matt had picked five so-called Anglo-Scots for his entire forward line, one of them was a kid, still four months short of his 19th birthday. Not only that but he had played fewer than 40 first-team games for his club – which was only an English Second Division side. Some very unkind things were churned out by the media at that time – I should know because I was that kid.

Walking out at Ninian Park wearing my Scotland shirt on 18 October 1958 was an experience that I shall never forget. I suppose it might have been better if it had been Hampden, but I would have played in a pub car park if it meant making my Scotland début. The Tartan Army was in great voice and here I was, playing among such great names as Eric Caldow, Bobby Collins, Tommy Docherty and Dave Mackay. I kept looking at them all and wondering if there had not been some mistake and that my name should not really have been on the team sheet.

The game kicked off at quite a pace and within a minute we were awarded a penalty. I was not asked to take it and I was glad because I was still very much on edge. Had I scored I would have settled immediately, but had I failed it could have ruined my game altogether. It was left to an older and wiser head than mine. Dave Mackay stepped up – and failed. He was big enough to just get on with the game.

If you look at the record books you will see that the final score was Wales 0, Scotland 3. You will also see that the goals were scored by Graham Leggat and yours truly. Yes, I scored on my début. We were ahead at half-time thanks to Graham Leggat. My 'goal' came in the second half and gave us a 2–0 lead. It was one of the most amazing goals with which I have ever been credited.

We were attacking and came close to scoring when Dave Bowen in the Welsh defence decided to give the loose ball a big boot to ease the pressure. I saw him preparing to swing his leg and, since I was not near enough to do anything constructive, I turned away. The next thing I knew was that the ball smacked against the back of my head and rebounded past Jack Kelsey, the Welsh goalkeeper. We were 2–0 ahead and the youngest Scottish international of the twentieth century had scored his first goal for his country. What a fluke!

On 5 November 1958 there were fireworks at Hampden when Scotland played Northern Ireland. Matt selected the same side that had beaten the Welsh, but I was given a slightly different role. I was instructed to man-mark the player whom Matt considered to be the most dangerous in the Irish side – Danny Blanchflower.

This was my first game at Hampden – my first ever senior football match on Scottish soil. Nearly 73,000 people turned up to watch and I could feel the hairs on the back of my neck bristle as we walked out into the vast arena. The noise was fantastic and it made you feel as if you were being carried along on a great wave.

Once the game was under way I stuck rigidly to my

instructions. I don't think I could have stayed closer to Danny if we had been Siamese twins. We took the lead early in the second half when David Herd scored. Bobby Collins made it 2–0 and we were coasting. I think it was when I was beginning to feel the pace that Danny Blanchflower found himself with a little space and Northern Ireland began to play. Under pressure, Eric Caldow scored an own goal, and then Jimmy McIlroy equalized. By the time the match ended at 2–2 we were quite pleased to hear the final whistle.

The fireworks came afterwards when Danny complained bitterly that I had kicked him all over the pitch. I laughed at him because, as far as I'm concerned, it is a man's game and if he couldn't take a little close attention from a teenager like me then he ought to be ashamed of himself. After all, wasn't this the great Danny Blanchflower? In hindsight I do have to admit that some of my tackles were a little over-zealous and I couldn't really blame him for complaining. Danny was a great player, one of the greatest ever. At that time, however, I was arrogant enough to laugh when he moaned about the treatment I had dished out to him. It's all part of growing up, I suppose.

An injury put my Scotland career on hold for six months, and I next pulled on the famous shirt in Aarhus against Jutland. It was a special representative game played in the Danish town but it did not count as an international. Even so, we fielded a strong side and drew 3–3 with me scoring our first goal.

A few days after that warm-up game we beat Holland 2–1 in Amsterdam. Bobby Collins and Graham Leggat once again performed the scoring honours. Also in the side was the great John White, who was a terrific player and was sadly missed when his life prematurely ended after he was struck by lightning on a golf course.

Our last game of that season was on 3 June 1959, when we lost 0–1 to Portugal, a side which included the marvellous Mário Coluna. My first season of international football drew to a close with four official appearances and one unofficial, two victories, two draws, one defeat and two goals. I was quite happy about it. My only disappointment was not to have been in the side which had been narrowly beaten 1–0 by England. I couldn't wait to get into one of those games.

In those days the British Championship was still alive and Scotland began the 1959–60 season with a trip to Belfast. I was in the side and quite annoyed that I didn't get on the scoresheet as we won 4–0. At home to Wales a month later, in November 1959, we drew 1–1 – and again I failed to score. I was continually being told that I was playing well and I continued to be selected, but when you are accustomed to scoring goals it is a little worrying when you fail to do so.

In April 1960 I was thrilled to be selected to play against England at Hampden. At last I was to have a crack at the Auld Enemy. Just a few hundred short of 130,000 packed into the mighty stadium for the contest. I had never seen so many people in one place. With the famous Hampden Roar urging us on we had England on the ropes for most of the game. We led 1–0 at half-time thanks to a Graham Leggat goal, but we just could not get the ball into the net a second time and, when Bobby Charlton scored from the penalty spot at the other end, I felt cheated. This should have been a great victory but instead we had to settle for the draw. I was determined to do better if ever I played against England again.

A month after that match we were at home to Poland in a friendly. They beat us 3–2 but there was some consolation in that I scored our first goal. Ian St John scored the other. We seemed to be on a bad run after that. At the end of May we began a three-match tour with a 1–4 defeat in Austria. My own tour ended almost as soon as it began. Alex Young replaced me when I was injured in the Austria game, and I did not recover in time to play again until the following season. Meanwhile Scotland drew 3–3 with Hungary and then lost 2–4 to Turkey.

It was another six months before my next Scotland game. To be precise it was 9 November 1960 and we were on the trail of the British Championship as it was then. I was disappointed when the annual competition between the home nations ceased to exist but I think it was probably well past its sell-by date. With today's integration of players from all over the world there isn't the same magic about the home nations playing each other – though I think the England–Scotland games could still pull in the crowds and stir up a few passions.

My first game back for Scotland was at Hampden against Northern Ireland, which gave me the chance to renew my acquaintance with Danny Blanchflower. This time he was having to keep an eye on me instead of the other way about. If my memory serves me correctly I think this was also the first full international for Jim Baxter, although you would never have known it. He had all the confidence and cheek of a seasoned international, both in the dressing room before the game and out on the pitch in the heat of the contest. We beat Northern Ireland 5–2.

Ralph Brand was also making his Scotland début and he did so in style, hitting two goals which brought an extra cheer from his Rangers fans. I scored one, Alex Young also scored one and Eric Caldow converted a penalty. It was a satisfying result and when we trooped off the pitch we were all smiles, completely unaware of the slaughter that lay ahead of us in the spring of 1961.

Ian McColl became manager of Scotland after Andy Beattie resigned to concentrate on his club activities. Ian was in an unenviable position. Not only was he still a Rangers player, but his appointment was solely on a match-by-match basis and, to be honest, he was there more as a coach than as a selector. The powers-that-be at the Scottish Football Association did not want to give up their slice of the action. I would not have liked to be in Ian's situation.

Though my boss at City, Les McDowall, was less than happy at the possibility of not having me in the side for a crucial League match against West Ham, my mind was made up that, if I was wanted by Scotland for the game against England at

Wembley in April 1961, wild horses would not stop me from being there.

England were on a roll when we met them. Earlier in the season they had already beaten Northern Ireland 5–2, Luxembourg 9–0, Spain 4–2 and Wales 5–1. Their form continued after they had played against us as they went on to beat Mexico 8–0. If it seems that I am reluctant to get round to talking about the match, those who recall the game will probably understand why.

There were mitigating circumstances since we did have several key players injured, including John White and Bill Brown. Frank Haffey was brought back to play in goal. The Celtic man was an excellent keeper but his only previous international experience was a 1–1 home draw against England a year earlier. I think that the big difference between the two sides was that England had a settled team which played like a club side, whereas we were a disjointed set of individuals who looked as if we had met only a few minutes before the match.

Bobby Robson set the ball rolling for England when he scored after nine minutes. The Tartan Army fell silent. This was not how it was supposed to be. There were almost 100,000 at Wembley that day and the Scots were the loudest as usual, but the English fans found their voices after Robson's goal and the atmosphere, which had already been intense, now became electrifying. It was almost as if something special was expected. Jimmy Greaves – who else? – made it 2–0 after 20 minutes and then, nine minutes after that, he scored again. I don't know why England did not score a lot more before half-time. We were there for the taking but the scoreline remained the same.

Our dressing room was more than a little animated during half-time. We were not just in disarray on the pitch, for those few minutes we were in a state off it as well. Blame was being handed around as if it was a grenade with the pin removed. We managed to pull ourselves together, though, and some team spirit began to spread through the camp. We realized that all was not lost and that we could get back into the game if we were prepared to give it a real shot. By the time we went back on to the pitch we were much more fired up than we had been at the start of the match.

The second half was not very old when Dave Mackay sent in a flying long shot which left Ron Springett in the England goal floundering. The ball thumped into the back of the net and the Tartan Army leapt to its feet as one. We gained a lot of confidence from that and it was not long before Davie Wilson scored our second with a terrific diving header. England were reeling and the scene was set for one of the greatest comebacks in the history of the game.

It didn't happen. England stormed back and were awarded a free-kick near our penalty area. To this day it seems to us that Jimmy Greaves gained an unfair advantage by taking the free-kick several yards nearer to the goal than he should have done. The referee must have had some mud in his eye for a moment and, from that kick, the ball found its way to Bryan Douglas, who made it 4–2. We were very disappointed because it seemed such an injustice.

We fell apart after that and England took full advantage of the situation. Bobby Smith made it 5–2 with 18 minutes left and, even when Pat Quinn scored for us, it didn't seem to matter any more. Johnny Haynes scored twice in less than two minutes, Jimmy Greaves completed his hat-trick, and Bobby Smith made it 9–3. It was a result that went down in history for all the wrong reasons from a Scottish viewpoint. While Johnny Haynes, the England captain, was being carried off the pitch shoulder-high and their goalkeeper Ron Springett was hurrying away to see his newborn daughter, Frank Haffey was in tears. I think we were all close to tears in our morgue of a dressing room, but Frank gave way to his. He never played for Scotland again.

As for me, well I think I must have shouldered some of the blame because I was dropped for the next three internationals, which were all World Cup qualifiers. In my absence, Scotland beat the Republic of Ireland 4–1 at Hampden and then 3–0 in Dublin. Czechoslovakia proved to be a tougher nut to crack, though, and we were hammered 0–4 in Bratislava. That was the last international of the 1960–61 season and I hoped that perhaps I would be back for another chance the following season.

Our 1961–62 campaign coincided with my move to Italy. I was now an international player in a different sense – a Scot who had moved to Italy from England. I was recalled to the Scotland side for the first international of the new season, a World Cup qualifier at home to Czechoslovakia, to be played under new floodlights. This was a vital match because we needed the points to stand a chance of qualifying. The Czechs would have been happy with a draw and we fully expected that they would come to Hampden to throw up a defensive wall, but we wanted to avenge the 0–4 defeat in Bratislava four months earlier.

There was a fierce wind blowing that night and it was a swirler, which seemed to favour the Czechs slightly. Once again Hampden was in good voice, although there was a stunned silence after just six minutes when Kvasnak put the Czechs ahead. It was a well-worked goal but we were in no mood to applaud it. Our heads did not go down and we set about getting an equalizer. The Czechs played imaginative and creative football and did not go heavy on defence. It was end-to-end stuff and everyone who was there said it was a great game to watch. Personally I found it very hard work.

We were nearly midway through the first half when a John White cross caught the Czech defence in two minds and I back-headed the ball to Ian St John who had no hesitation in heading home under the Czech goalie. Hampden went crazy! The score remained at 1–1 for the rest of the first half but, on the six-minute mark of the second half, the Czechs struck again when a long clearance found Scherer completely on his own. He trotted about 40 yards and easily slipped the ball past Bill Brown to make it 2–1.

The Tartan Army would not allow us to get depressed, though. They roared us on to greater effort and, sure enough, we equalized again. Another excellent cross from John White came to me and I stabbed the ball into the net. We worked even harder then, although heavy rain made the conditions poor and these were not helped by a bit of Czech tackling which flattened a few people. Finally, with seven minutes left, I took another great pass from John White, slipped a couple of threshing-machine type tackles, and put the ball past Schroiff in the Czech goal. The score stayed at 3–2 and there were great celebrations after the game.

We needed the Republic of Ireland to take at least one point from their two games with the Czechs, but they failed and we had to meet Czechoslovakia once again in a group decider in Brussels. There were two more international fixtures before that match and I did not appear in either of them. My contract with Torino allowed me to be released only for World Cup games for my country and even then, when I played against Czechoslovakia, the Scottish Football Association were forced to insure me for £200,000.

I missed the 6–1 win over Northern Ireland in Belfast and the 2–0 win over Wales at Hampden, but I was allowed out of Italy once again for the decider against Czechoslovakia in Brussels. The pitch was wet and heavy and once again we were without several of our key men. Two players were making their débuts, Hugh Robertson and goalkeeper Eddie Connachan, both of whom in fact only won one cap each. We had two others, Ian Ure and Alec Hamilton, who were making only their second international appearances and we were facing a full-strength Czech side with a wealth of experience.

We were leading 2–1 with only eight minutes left, thanks to two goals from Ian St John. Then the Czechs 'equalized' with a 'goal' that was dodgy to say the least. The ball hit the underside of the bar, bounced down and came out. The referee gave the goal but there was absolutely no way that he could have had clear vision and, after all, the laws of the game state that the whole ball must be seen to cross the line. That goal led to extra time and it proved to be too much for us. We hit the woodwork, had one or two players scythed down without compensation, and conceded two more goals. It was a sickener, but at least we had the consolation of seeing the side that had stopped us qualifying for the 1962 World Cup go all the way to the final.

There was not another international until April 1962 when England were visitors to Hampden. To my surprise Torino agreed to release me for the game. There were not too many weeks left of the Italian League season and I think they knew that I was looking for an escape route. We were still smarting from that last encounter with England, and the smell of revenge hung heavy in the air. We were determined not to lose face in front of the 132,441-strong Hampden crowd and a goal from Davie Wilson in the first half and another penalty from Eric Caldow in the second did the trick. We may not have outclassed England but I think we outplayed them and we won. That was the important thing!

My next Scotland outing was in the following October. By that time I was playing in England once again and there was no problem with my availability. I scored in our 3–2 win over Wales in Cardiff and then, in November, I hit four as we beat Northern Ireland 5–1. I was very happy to be back in Britain and I think it gave my football a new lease of life. I no longer felt so restricted.

In April 1963 we were on the way to Wembley once again to meet England who, no doubt, wanted to avenge their defeat at Hampden the previous year, and were still living off their 9–3 win the year before that. Nobody gave us much of a chance of avoiding defeat – except we ourselves, that is. Ian McColl was still in charge of Scotland and nobody wanted success at Wembley more than he did. By the time we walked out of the famous Wembley tunnel, we would have taken on any team in the world – preferably all of them, one after the other.

Jim Baxter loved to turn it on against England, and this game was no exception. He ran rings round the England defenders and added insult to injury by scoring our first goal. By the time he had made it 2–0 with a penalty before half-time, our supporters were having the time of their lives. England threw everything at us in the second half and pulled back a goal through Bryan Douglas, but we held on and even came close to adding to our score a few times before the final whistle went and we had pulled off a memorable victory. On the down side, we had lost Eric Caldow with a broken leg, but we all – including Eric – went home very happy. We had won the British Championship but, even more importantly, we had beaten England in their own back yard.

A month later we had another memorable game, but this one was to be remembered for all the wrong reasons. It was supposed to be a friendly but Austria's manager, Karl Decker, set the ball rolling before the match when he said some very insulting things about Scottish football. Added to that it appeared that he was taking the mickey in his side's pre-match training, and there were other arguments going on behind the scenes about the number of substitutes to be allowed.

Ian McColl had worked hard to have us focused for the game and, within three minutes, I had the ball in the net only to be told that I was off-side. I still think that the referee, Jim Finney, was wrong. There was just over a quarter of an hour gone when Jimmy Milar and Davie Wilson worked a piece of magic that clearly showed how well they played together in their Rangers shirts. Wilson scored, and then they did a repeat performance about ten minutes later which put us into a convincing 2–0 lead.

Within minutes of that all hell was let loose. The Austrians began to put the boot in and, when Finney cautioned Nemec, the Austrian striker went crazy and had a right go back at the referee. The upshot was that Nemec received his marching orders. Everyone was stunned. The Austrian manager and his colleagues ran on to the pitch and Finney was suddenly surrounded by a seething mass of irate Austrians. At that stage Finney threatened to abandon the game but peace was somehow restored. A few minutes later I scored to make it 3–0.

The Austrians' attitude worsened in the second half. They kicked anything that moved and were ridiculously petulant, engaging in time-wasting even though they were three goals down. I scored another goal and that seemed to aggravate matters. Even when they pulled one back their mood did not seem to improve. Their centre-half, Gletchner, pole-axed Jimmy Milar and was cautioned, and just after that their inside-forward committed the foul of the night when he tried a bit of tree-felling on Willie Henderson. The referee sent him off immediately. Once again there was a pitch invasion by the Austrian officials and it took five minutes to settle things down.

Within seconds of the restart, I was on the receiving end of another scything tackle from Linhart. The referee blew his whistle and, when I looked up, I saw him walking off the pitch. Nobody knew what was happening. He disappeared down the tunnel and we were left waiting until Willie Allan, the SFA secretary, came out on to the pitch and told us the game was over. The referee had abandoned it with just over ten minutes' playing time left.

Jim Finney later explained that the tackle on me had been the final straw. He felt that if he had not abandoned the game, someone would have been seriously injured and that there might well have been crowd trouble as well. Officials from both parties did not agree, but FIFA fully backed the referee in his decision and he went on to become one of the world's senior officials. I'm inclined to agree with Jock Stein, who was reported to have said at the time, 'For too long British teams have gone abroad to be pushed around, booted all over the park by foreigners who disobey the rules. I know that Mr Finney has been criticized but, to my mind, he showed great courage.' As always, Jock Stein told it the way it was.

Some interesting games followed that one. We lost 3–4 to Norway but I had the personal consolation of scoring a hat-trick. Then we lost to the Republic of Ireland 0–1 but returned to form with a 6–2 victory in Spain in which I hit two. That was another game to remember. In my next international I scored four as we gained a 6–1 revenge over Norway at home. Seven goals in two matches against the Norwegians gave me something of a reputation in Scandinavia and I still get mail from there reminding me of those two games.

A 1–0 win over England at Hampden in April 1964 was enjoyed by all of us and the even bigger crowd of 133,245. Alan Gilzean scored the winner that day. Later that year we were back in World Cup action with high hopes of qualifying. We were especially keen because the 1966 World Cup was to be played in England, and that was about as near as we were likely to get to playing in the finals 'at home'.

Our campaign started well enough with home and away wins over Finland and a draw away to Poland. Just before the game in Poland, Ian McColl quit as manager. I think he was pushed rather than jumped, which was a surprise really because his record had been pretty good. Jock Stein stepped in as caretaker manager and that meant a few changes of tack. Not long after the start of the 1965-66 season we faced Poland at home and lost 1–2. Our chances of qualifying had gone from looking good to being in the balance. It was not the manager's fault, it was just a run of circumstances. Things looked a lot better after we had played Italy at home in November 1965. A John Greig goal gave us a deserved victory. I had been dropped for that game because I was going through a bit of a quiet patch, but I was as thrilled as if I had been playing.

The possibility of playing in the World Cup tournament was starting to look very good once again. We had beaten Italy once and we felt that we could beat them again – or at the very least force a draw and corner them into a play-off. I don't know if I would have been selected for this one but injury ruled me out anyway, so I had to sit through the game in utter frustration as the Italians gained the victory they needed. It was only in the last quarter of an hour that they really looked safe as their 1–0 lead had been flattering to them up to then. It was annoying to think that we were not going to feature in World Cup '66, and all the more so because the Auld Enemy were hosts.

After our defeat by Italy in December 1965 we went through a really bad year. England beat us 4–3 at Hampden in April 1966. I was back for that one and scored, but this was my only international appearance of that year. In fact, I did not pull on a Scotland shirt again until April 1967 for the visit to Wembley – a game I would not have missed for the world.

England had won the World Cup in 1966 and had not been beaten since. The English newspapers were full of stories by this expert and that talking about how many goals England would put past Scotland. We were no-hopers. We had won only one game in the last 16 months and would be no match for the reigning world champions.

We had other ideas, of course. Billy Bremner was quietly determined and, as he sat in the dressing room, he looked grittier than I had ever seen him. Jimmy Baxter kept talking about how he was going to make fools of the England defenders and was actually taking bets on how many players he would 'nutmeg' – especially Ray Wilson, that tough England defender. The spirit in the dressing room was just amazing. It was our manager Bobby Brown's first match in charge and he surprised everyone by selecting Ronnie Simpson for his début. The Celtic goalkeeper was 36 years old, but Bobby assured everybody that he was ' a great man in a crisis'.

I don't know about a crisis but he certainly had a great game. We hurt England very deeply that day. Jim Baxter was as good as his word and put on an exhibition the like of which has not been seen at Wembley since. Not only did he win his 'nutmeg' bet but, at one stage, he actually started juggling with the ball as if he were in a training session. The vast Tartan Army in the near-capacity crowd absolutely loved it. I scored our first goal when I pounced on a rebound, and in the second half Bobby Lennox made it 2–0. Jack Charlton scored for England with six minutes left and then Jim McCalliog made it 3–1 to us. Even when Geoff Hurst scored another late England goal, there was no question but that we were going to record a terrific victory. It was 3–2, and could have been 5–2 but for some great goal-keeping by Gordon Banks. As far as we were concerned we were now the new World Champions.

My international career continued through the rest of the 1960s and into the 1970s. There were, of course, good days and bad days. Failing to qualify for the 1970 World Cup was a bad day. I was beginning to wonder if I would ever play in a World Cup tournament. I had probably only one more chance, at the 1974 competition that was to be held in West Germany. But there was no guarantee that I would be selected, even if Scotland did manage to qualify.

One of my greatest experiences was to play against Brazil in the mighty Maracaña Stadium. We were there for a summer tournament in 1972 and, after drawing with Yugoslavia and Czechoslovakia, we faced a Brazilian side which included such legendary names as Jairzinho and Tostão. It was Jairzinho who scored the only goal of the game, but we came away with our heads held high in the knowledge that we had almost taken the greatest team in the world to a points decision.

That trip to Brazil proved to be a good launching pad for Scotland's opening matches for the 1974 World Cup because the team beat Denmark both home and away. I was not involved in either game and in fact I missed the next few internationals. I returned in September 1973 and took part in the 2–1 win over Czechoslovakia at Hampden. At the start of the campaign Tommy Docherty had been in charge but, by the time the game against the Czech side was imminent, Willie Ormond had taken over the reins. Amazingly it had been 12 years to the day since I had scored twice against Czechoslovakia in that play-off in Belgium. I did not score in the 1973 game but I enjoyed playing a part in the victory. It was a rough match and the 100,000 crowd seemed to enjoy every moment of it. There was a great roar when the final whistle went because we knew that, even if we lost the return, Scotland would be taking part in the 1974 World Cup. To add to the fun, England had failed to qualify.

I did not assume that I would be in the squad – but I hoped, I really hoped. It had always been an ambition of mine to play at least one game on the greatest football stage of them all. At the end of the season we still had to play the British Championship games against Northern Ireland, Wales and England. We lost 0–1 at home to the Irishmen and I was substituted by Joe Jordan. I was not called up for the 2–0 win over Wales and I also failed to take part in the 2–0 win over England. I knew that two days after the England game the Scotland squad would be announced and I had virtually given up hope of being included.

It was a great surprise when the news came through on Monday morning that I had indeed been picked. Willie Ormond had decided to stick with the squad that had taken part in the British Championship and that included me. I could not stop smiling. It was brilliant news.

I did not take part in any of the friendly matches prior to the World Cup tournament but, on 14 June 1974, I pulled on the Scotland shirt that meant so much to me and went out to face the unknown quantity of Zaire in our opening game. Brazil and Yugoslavia were also in our group and so we realized that it was not going to be an easy task.

Nobody knew anything about Zaire and how they would play. They were considered to be the ultimate underdogs. Today of course, everyone knows that African countries are no push-overs, but in those days it was expected that we would get double figures against them. Because we failed to do so we came in for a lot of stick. It was easier for those that followed because they were able to study how Zaire had played against us. We did not have that advantage and so were probably guilty of being a little too tentative in our approach. Once we had got the measure of them we won comfortably with a 2–0 scoreline that could have been much greater but for the number of times we hit the woodwork, or were foiled by a very good goalkeeper.

Peter Lorimer and Joe Jordan scored our goals. I would have

liked to have had my name on the scoresheet because it was a very special match for me. Not only did I fulfil my dream of playing in the World Cup but, as it turned out, it was also my last game for Scotland. Even more than that, it was my last first-class game.

Scotland drew 0–0 with Brazil and then 1–1 with Yugoslavia. There was an outside chance that we might qualify for the next stage until Brazil scored their third goal against Zaire towards the end of the game. That goal was enough to see them through at our expense. We returned home, the only unbeaten side in the entire tournament. We were fêted and congratulated for our performance and it was nice to hear so many people saying so many lovely things. For me, however, there was a tinge of sadness. After 55 appearances and 30 goals – plus one unofficial goal in an unofficial international – it was all over.

5

ITALIANO

Well, that was Scotland. But now let's turn the clock back to my transfer from Manchester City to Italy. I would not go as far as saying that it was a mistake because it was certainly an experience that must have been of some benefit to me in my life but, as adventures go, I don't think it rates as highly as bungee-jumping without the elastic.

In my first club game in Italy I was still wearing a Manchester City shirt. It was June 1961 and the administrative formalities were awaiting completion when I travelled out with City to play a friendly against Torino. I suppose it was one of football's worst-kept secrets that I was about to join them, but everyone went along with the farce of keeping it quiet. This was partly because there was some dispute over whether or not I had been clear to join Torino. I knew that the piece of paper that I had signed regarding joining Inter was totally meaningless. Had the club not been interested in me they would have simply ripped it up and there would have been nothing I could have done about it, but it was far from clear how Inter did feel about the situation.

When I set foot in the aeroplane taking us for the friendly with Torino I was still a Manchester City player. By the time I stepped off the plane in Turin I had virtually changed camps as it had been announced at an impromptu press conference during the flight that I was officially joining Torino. There was a great clamouring of the press, especially the Italian press, and it reached amazing proportions after the news broke because Inter threw their hat into the ring and claimed that I was their player. The two clubs had a public row as I sat in the middle wondering exactly which shirt I was going to be wearing the following season. At this stage I half-suspected that it might still be a Manchester City one.

The Italian media were as demonstrative then as they are now and I was besieged. It was my first experience of being the subject of a press stampede and I could not say that I enjoyed it very much. Not being able to speak the language didn't help either. It's quite bad enough being misquoted in your own language but when you are misquoted in someone else's it adds extra complications.

We played the friendly ... well, most of it anyway. The match had to be abandoned because of a torrential downpour. Before it was called off I scored, and that was to be my last goal for Manchester City at that time and my first on Italian soil. After the game I said my farewells because I was staying in Italy while my former team-mates travelled home. I still had to sign a few things, have a medical and meet some people. The Italian season had officially ended but there were one or two games to be played in order to complete the fixtures. I was therefore able to watch some Italian League football and engage in a few training sessions with my new club. I also had time to take a look at Turin.

If you have thought about visiting Turin but never got around to it, I urge you to. It is a lovely city, both historic and picturesque, which nestles in the comfortable shadows of the Italian Alps. The one major scar in the history of Turin – or more especially Torino football club – is that in 1949 the side was involved in a plane crash and, just like in Manchester United's tragedy at Munich almost a decade later, the first team was decimated. No fewer than 18 players were killed in the disaster and it feels as if that part of the city is still in mourning. Prior to the accident Torino had been champions for four successive seasons, and now, some half a century later, the football club is still striving to recapture the tremendous status it had previously held. Since then they have been champions just once, in 1976.

As I went through the formalities of joining Torino the row between them and Inter continued to blaze. Gigi Peronace assured me that there was no problem and acted as my interpreter, a role which he fulfilled for both myself and Joe Baker throughout our time in Italy. I also received assurances from Angelo Filippone, then president of Torino. Although I was keen to see the matter resolved I was not losing any sleep over it. I knew I would be playing for someone when the new season started. I hoped it was going to be Torino, but I did not at any stage think I would be out of work. The nail-biting was all down to them.

After I had completed the arrangements I returned to Scotland to spend some time with my family. Before I left, I was told to relax and have a good holiday and that by the time I returned the dispute would be over and I would be able to concentrate on my new career with Torino. That reassurance was mostly correct.

While I was back in Scotland the dispute was settled and Inter looked elsewhere for British players, finally signing Gerry Hitchens from Aston Villa. With Joe Baker and myself at Torino, John Charles at Juventus, Eddie Firmani at Sampdoria, plus of course Jimmy Greaves at AC Milan, the Italian League was starting to look rather similar to the Premiership of the last few seasons.

The only part of the reassurance that was not correct was that the Italian press continued to harp on about the confusion for some time. I'm not sure whether or not it worked in my favour that I could not speak Italian. I was incessantly asked for interviews and, while I did my best, I still managed to be voted the most uncooperative player in Italian football by one major newspaper, *Tutto Sport*. Meanwhile, others showered me with praise and at one stage the Italian sportswriters named me their No. 1 player. I think they either loved me or hated me; there was no in-between. I never hated them. I have always respected the fact that journalists have a job to do the same as everyone else and, if they go about it in a civilized manner, a good time can be had by all. If they get pushy, try to put words in your mouth, or just deliberately misquote you, then I have no time for them – be they British, Italian or any other nationality. I felt exactly the same in Italy during the 1960s. I would treat the 'gentlemen of the press' as gentlemen and the gutter-rakers as gutter-rakers, but when you do that you always upset someone and that is why my relationship with the Italian media was so stormy.

The Italian press was only one of the irritations of being in Italy. When Joe Baker and I reported for training about six weeks before the start of the Italian season, we gradually began to realize that this paradise to which we had travelled had a few hidden mines that nobody had warned us about. Most of them were financial mines which regularly blew up in our faces.

First there was the saga of the hotel bill. Joe and I had been promised accommodation supplied by the club, but this was very slow in coming, so we had to spend the first few months of our Italian adventure living in an hotel. When we were presented with hotel bills of several hundred pounds, we refused to pay. We were under the impression that, since the club had not yet supplied us with the promised accommodation, they would pick up the tab for the hotel in which we were being forced to stay. We were told that we had got it all wrong and there was a huge row. We stuck to our guns, though, and eventually the club was forced, very reluctantly, to pay up.

Another dodgy payment situation arose over my signing-on fee. I had received a third before I returned to Italy for the start of the season and was supposed to receive the rest in two instalments during the season. I felt I would have to keep an eye on the situation as it did not look too promising. To cut a long story short, I never did receive those two payments.

There was also a varied system of fines in Italian football of which we were not aware. When Joe Baker was sent off on one occasion he was fined by the Italian FA, he was fined by the club, he was suspended and therefore lost the chance to win bonuses during that time and, after he had sat down to work it all out, he told me that he was at least £500 out of pocket, which was a lot of money then, for what was probably a refereeing error in the first place.

Our annoyance at these various impositions was usually taken out on Gigi Peronace, who was the nearest thing either of us had to an agent. We nearly reduced him to tears a few times and, while I have sometimes felt some remorse at that, it has to be said that we were real innocents in Italy in those days and unexpected deductions came as a big shock to us.

It was late August when the Italian season kicked off. We had been training in the heat but we were still not fully prepared for the heat during a game. It did not help that we were based in northern Italy and our first game was in the south close to the Mediterranean. The sun was beating down as we took the field against Sampdoria, and by midway through the second half I felt as if I had just crawled on my hands and knees across the Sahara desert. Any thoughts which I may have had of scoring on my début were nothing more than a mirage. We lost 0–2 and when we got back into the dressing room I was totally dehydrated and just wanted to be allowed to die peacefully. There were probably vultures wheeling in the sky overhead. It was a harsh lesson but it made me realize that I was going to have to pace myself much better.

According to the press reports I had quite a good game even though we lost. I had to take their word for it because, quite honestly, I could not remember too much about it. I remembered our first home match, though. The visitors were Lanerossi Vicenza and there was a capacity crowd to see the new boys in action for the first time. I think we succeeded in giving them what they were hoping for because there was a standing ovation at half-time. We were well in control and by halfway through the second half we were leading 3–1 and coasting to our first victory. Joe Baker had scored two great goals and I had added the third.

Throughout the game, both Joe and myself had been kicked, slapped, spat at, had our hair pulled, and endured just about everything you could think of from over-zealous opponents. I was half-expecting someone to run on to the pitch with a violin case, take a machine-gun out, and shoot us both. There was one guy in particular who had done nothing but try to maim Joe Baker from the moment the referee started the game. In the end Joe could not stand it any longer and lashed out. It was not a vicious assault. Joe just flung his arm at the player to stop him coming in with yet another kick at his calf-muscle.

The Italian went down and rolled around as if Joe had hit him with a hammer and then knifed him for good measure. I had never seen anything quite like it – except perhaps in a film where people are shot at and turn cartwheels and somersaults before they finally bite the dust. I was half-laughing at the Italian's antics when I suddenly realized that Joe was in trouble for the incident. I was stunned when the referee showed him the red card. The other guy opened one eye to make sure that his drama was having the right results and I felt like closing it for him. It was a sick joke to see the victim being sent off while the hired assassin was getting away scot-free, if you'll pardon the expression.

The furore that followed completely unsettled our side and the visitors scored twice to end the match at 3–3. They were delighted with that, but I was fuming. As I sat in the dressing room I was already beginning to wish that I had never agreed to come to Italy. The seeds of discontent had been firmly sown in that game. If this was what Italian football was really like, they could keep it. I admit to having been tempted by the money and the opportunity to get away from Maine Road, but the word 'mistake' kept coming into my mind.

By the time we were ready to play our next game I had calmed down a little and decided that perhaps that little incident was just an isolated case and that most matches would not be like that. How wrong can you be? Most matches were exactly like that. I found, and I know that others who were there also agree, that Italian football was not at all what we had expected. True, there were some very skilful players and the approach to the game was a lot more professional than back in Britain. Italian football, or at least its image, oozed class. However, those players who did not have the breathtaking skills of the few made up for their lack by kicking lumps out of everyone else.

There was hardly a match in which I did not find myself getting elbowed, pinched, punched and generally knocked about. I could take care of myself but it is difficult to play your game and keep your balance when you are constantly fending off someone who has been told to mark you – and is taking his instructions a little too literally. There were times when it would have been easier to count the areas of unblemished skin rather than the bruises. If you responded like for like, then you immediately set off a storm of protest from the opposition as your assailant rolled around as if his career had just been ended. Once he had gained the referee's sympathy he would get up and trot away without so much as a care in the world.

Personally I found it disgusting. When I see players copying that sort of behaviour nowadays it makes me very angry. I hate diving, I hate the dramatics, and I hate it when commentators talk about someone 'winning a penalty' or 'winning a free-kick'. When I was playing, you were awarded free-kicks and penalties when someone broke the rules in trying to stop you from scoring a goal. It is very sad that today's game seems to consider that part of a forward's skill is the ability to 'win' free-kicks and penalties. It made me sick in Italy and it still makes me sick today whenever and wherever I see it.

I was not the only one having a bad time in Italy. Joe Baker was unhappy of course, and so was Jimmy Greaves, who could not wait to get away from AC Milan. Gerry Hitchens also told me that he was not very happy with Inter Milan. It seemed that if you were a defender then life was not so bad, but if you were a forward you were expected to go through hell every time you played. Added to the strange aspects of our treatment off the pitch, the picture was looking more drab than it had at first been painted.

I know I must be sounding rather miserable again. I have already written about the down-side of Manchester City and now, it seems, it is the turn of Italian football. However, in neither case was it all negative. We had a few laughs with our Torino team-mates, who were not a bad bunch of guys. Our captain was Enzo Bearzot, a great player and leader, who rose to even greater fame some years later when the Italian national side managed by him won the World Cup in 1982.

Training sessions were not only enjoyable but I knew they were doing a lot of good. Our manager, or coach as the Italians prefer to call them, was Beniamino Santos, an Argentinian who had joined Torino as a player shortly after the club's horrific air-crash. He had been in charge of the youth section, but had been recently promoted to manager. He was what we would call a 'tracksuit manager'. He liked to work with the players himself rather than just get progress reports from a handful of staff.

The sessions were a revelation. There was not a lot of shouting and talking – all the exercises were controlled by whistles. The emphasis was not on stamina as it was in Britain. Santos liked to have his players quick and nippy rather than capable of plodding on for hours on end, and he scheduled his training programmes that way. You would start off with jogging and exercises and then he would call out players two at a time to concentrate on ball work. Basically, the way the programmes were organized, everyone had what they personally needed rather than being just a part of a squad going through the same exercises as everyone else.

Every training session was watched by about 5,000 fans, and that too took a bit of getting used to. In Britain you might get the occasional passer-by who would stop for a moment as they were walking their dog, but in Italy going to watch the training was second only to watching a live match. After a session you would find yourself surrounded by fans wanting to know if you were fit to play the next game, or if there was any truth in the story that so-and-so was carrying an injury.

The fanatical support did not end there. We had plenty of time on our hands as we were encouraged to relax and enjoy life as much as possible. Joe Baker and I knocked about together quite a lot, as you would expect, but it was difficult to go anywhere without being besieged by fans. If you went to a restaurant you would find a queue of autograph hunters at your table, or faces pressed against the window as they watched you eat. If you went shopping you had to allow more than twice the time it would normally take because people wanted to talk to you about football first, then perhaps have their photograph taken with you, before they would serve you with what you wanted.

If you decided to hang around at the club during your time off, you would be besieged by a different kind of supporter – the directors. Everyone wanted to be your best pal and to advise you on every move you made – whether it be on the pitch or investing your salary. It was difficult to be constantly polite to everyone, but we did our best and kept telling ourselves that most of those who wanted to talk to us were genuine fans of the club and deserved our time and attention.

After a couple of months we were involved in our first local derby. In Turin there are two major clubs, Torino and Juventus. I knew all about rivalries in Britain between clubs like Manchester United and City, Liverpool and Everton and, of course, the Old Firm games in Glasgow – but my first Italian derby match was something quite amazing.

After losing on the opening day we had not been beaten again and had put a good run of results together. We were looking good prospects for the Italian championship, which only added to the rising temperature in Turin and, when the big day arrived, the massive Stadio Comunale was packed, with many more locked outside. Juventus easily had the upper hand in local derbies and it was expected that our good run would come to an abrupt end on that day.

As it happened, Torino played out of their skins and we beat Juventus 1–0, with Joe Baker scoring the only goal of the game. It was a brilliant result and the Torino fans went absolutely crazy. The streets were so full of their partying that it was a laborious job for our coach to leave the stadium and travel the short distance to our own ground where our private cars were parked. On the way we were held up by a funeral procession. Knowing what life was like in Italy it worried me for a moment that the coffins I could see being carried shoulder-high might have contained some supporters killed in a crowd crush. I had no need to worry. As our coach drove by it became obvious to us all that the coffins, which were draped in Juventus colours, were simply a part of our own fans' celebrations.

We extended our unbeaten run to 13 games and you might think that the earlier desire to return home would have waned a little. But it wasn't so. Each game meant the same inquisition of kicking and punching, and off-the-field negotiations over bonuses and fines continued week after week. After living for months in the hotel where we did not feel at all at home, we were finally handed the keys to our apartment. It was the first thing in luxury and security, but still we did not feel at home. It was as if we had moved from a luxury hotel to luxury self-catering.

The battle against boredom was sometimes worse than getting kicked all over the park during a game. Television was useless to us and you can only spend so much time reading yesterday's English newspapers. Going out meant that you ran the gauntlet of fans and press and so Joe and I began to feel more like cell-mates than team-mates.

We never shirked our work and we never shirked from saying our piece either. The Italians must have thought us total pains in the rear, but we knew that if we did not stand up for ourselves, nobody else would bother on our behalf. There was even an occasion when Joe went on hunger-strike. The team used to stay at an hotel up in the mountains for several days before each game, and it was a bit like being sent to Alcatraz. There was nothing to do except train, eat and sleep. Nobody liked it, but the Italians kept their mouths shut. Not Joe Baker, though. He had a justifiable moan to Gigi Peronace and decided there and then that he would go on hunger-strike until we went back to Turin, never to return to this hotel. Gigi did not really believe him until Joe failed to turn up at mealtime. Then Gigi explained to our manager and lengthy discussions were held. To our delight and amazement we were told that we would not be returning to the hotel. Joe came off his hunger-strike and played a blinder in the next game.

That was not the end of the matter because there were various altercations between the management and the executives, and the press also got involved, though the players kept out of it. It was nothing to do with us, we innocently told everyone. Joe was more innocent than any of us – but to the rest of the lads he was a hero.

There were very few weeks when something controversial did not happen. On one occasion Joe and I went out on the town with two ladies, only to find out later that one of them had been paid by a press photographer to be there. Within a day or two a newspaper published photographs of Joe and his young lady in an amorous situation. The irony of it was that it was supposed to have been me, but Joe and I had swapped young ladies during the evening. Needless to say we were both in trouble with the club for allowing it to happen. In truth we had not seen any sign of the photographer.

On another occasion, Joe and I were taking a walk around Venice where we had gone for a game, when a press photographer started following us. Everywhere we went he was there. Every shop window we looked into, every time a pretty girl went past or a policeman was near us, we were aware of his camera clicking away. It was driving us crazy, but that photographer was completely undeterred and blatantly shadowed us every step of our way. Eventually, in our very limited Italian, we pleaded with him to leave us alone now that he had a fair batch of photographs. He just ignored us and continued taking pictures. The next thing I knew Joe had swung a punch and the guy hit the deck. Within seconds there was a crowd around us – and they were decidedly hostile. We managed to push our way free of them, but it was a close thing and to make matters worse the grapevine sent word like lightning back to the club and once again Baker and Law were in trouble with the bosses. Worse still, we were in trouble with the police.

We were taken to a police station and given the third degree. The photographer had been taken to hospital where it was found that he had not been badly hurt. Joe's punch had done little damage, but the photographer had hit the pavement face-first which made the injury look a lot worse. However, the wounds were only superficial. What we had not realized at the time was that this guy had a club foot – and he therefore easily won the sympathy vote. The consensus of opinion was that two foreigners had come to Venice and beaten up a crippled photographer. Nice one!

The upshot was that we had to pay him £1,000 in compensation. Joe was excluded from the match in Venice and lost more money because of that. We travelled to the game by motor launch along the famous canals and at every bridge there were home fans throwing things at us. By then I felt like jumping off the boat and swimming back to Scotland.

It did not get any better during the match either. With Joe sitting back at the hotel, I became the prime target for everyone who wanted to maim the foreign villain who had been unmercifully cruel to a poor, harmless and lame photographer. The home fans wanted blood – and nearly got it several times. We ended the game with a 1–0 victory in our pockets and the motor launch trip back to our hotel was an absolute nightmare. Once again the fans gathered on the bridges and the pelting that we had taken earlier now became such a bombardment that we had to seek refuge beneath our seats. I remember crouching down while this air-raid went on every time we passed under a bridge – and there seem to be hundreds of them in Venice. I looked around at everyone else also seeking safety under the seats and I began to wonder what the hell I was doing there.

Talking of hostile crowds, I did not realize what it would be like to play against Palermo – the heroes of Sicily, birthplace of the Mafia. I was amused when I heard that Sivori, one of our top players, refused even to travel to the game. Later I learned that when he had been playing for Juventus he had received death threats over an incident during a game against Palermo, and he had decided that there was no way he was going to find out whether those threats were real or not.

The match was one of the strangest experiences I have ever had. You could feel a solid wall of animosity coming from the terraces. There were no women, no children, just men – and all dressed near enough the same, in black. They just stared at you and it made you feel like each and every one of them was carrying a gun and deciding where to plant the bullet. Every time you went anywhere near the terraces missiles were hurled at you. I am not ashamed to admit that I was scared, very scared. I have seen plenty of hostile crowds in my time, but I have never experienced one quite like that. We lost the game by a single goal and I think we were all relieved when it was over. I dread to think what might have happened if we had had the nerve to win.

It was in February 1962 that the most unforgettable incident made its indelible mark on our lives. The club had provided us with a Fiat and most of our driving had been done by me, but Joe Baker decided that, if nothing else, he was going to enjoy having a dream car of his own and so he went out and bought this lovely Alfa Romeo. When my brother came to visit, we thought it would be a good opportunity for Joe to try out his new car, and he drove us to a restaurant up in the mountains where we had a light meal and a couple of drinks. To my dying day I will swear that we only had a couple of glasses of mild wine. We were certainly not drunk, as some people claimed later.

When we travelled back to Turin it was nearly midnight and we thought that we might go to a quiet club we had discovered near our apartment. On the way we had to go round a roundabout and, since Joe was still not used to driving on the right, he began to take it the British way. I quickly told him he was going the wrong way and, as he tried to rectify the situation, the car hit a high kerb and the next thing I knew I was in hospital. Apparently the Alfa Romeo had somersaulted several times. Joe had been thrown out and I had been flung across into the driver's seat, which had saved me as my side of the car had taken the greatest impact. My brother had been sitting in the back and did not have so much as a bruise.

Joe Baker was in a very bad way. His facial injuries were hideous and the doctors worked on him all night to try and patch him up. As it was, they did not hold out much hope for him and he was on the critical list. I was allowed to see him the following day and I thought he was going to die. When they told me what they had had to do to put him back together I felt decidedly sick. My own injuries were minor, the worst being a badly gashed hand which had been pierced by glass. Amazingly, a year later I was still having pain from that hand and, when I opened it up myself with a needle, I pulled out a piece of glass about a quarter of an inch long.

I was allowed home after I had seen Joe, and John Charles came over to see me at the apartment. He brought a pile of newspapers and, looking at the photographs of the car, I realized just how close to death I had been. John was absolutely brilliant to us during our time in Italy. He was well established there with Juventus and he liked the place. The Italians thought the world of him as well and he often helped us to keep our sanity by turning up just when we most needed a pal from Britain.

After a day or two I was able to resume training, but Joe remained in hospital of course. He improved after a few days but was convinced that I was dead. It was only when Gigi Peronace took me to see him that he cheered up a little and began his long road to recovery. He was on a drip for 42 days, which is a long time indeed in the career of a professional sportsman. The doctors were very good and they were certain that if he had not been such a fit footballer, Joe Baker would have died.

With our partnership at least suspended I got on with the job of playing my best for my club. My pal was not there now and I had to go it alone. I came in for even more stick from defenders but I gave as good as I got. On one occasion I probably gave a little more. We were playing against a small club called Spal and I was getting some aggravation from two of their players. I knew that the following day my legs would look as though I had bathed in Ribena. I took as much as I was prepared to take and then waited my chance to retaliate.

The referee was busy and the linesmen were also occupied. I spun round on one of the guys who had been using my legs for target practice and threw a great right hook at his jaw. He went down like they always do but, instead of rolling about to attract attention, he just stayed there with a trickle of blood coming from his mouth. I did not wait around but moved away to pretend innocence. Of course the crowd had seen the whole thing and went crazy – but the officials had seen nothing. The guy was stretchered off and regained consciousness a few minutes later. The referee, Mr Lo Bello, came over to me and in perfect English told me he had not seen what happened but could hazard a reasonable guess. I was told to watch it or he would send me off. I behaved myself after that and stayed on the pitch. I nearly wished he had sent me off because, as we left the field at the end of the game, a mob of Spal players threw punches at me in the tunnel. I avoided most of them and my team-mates surrounded me to get me safely to the dressing room. If they had been just a little slower, yours truly might well have been found hanging from a Spal flagpole.

Despite all these incidents I had become quite popular in my short time in Italy and, while the news reporters might have considered me to be some sort of foreign hooligan, the sports journalists were much kinder and said some nice things. I had not changed my mind about leaving at the earliest opportunity, though, and the prospect of returning to Britain was never far from my thoughts.

Back in November 1961 I had played for the Italian League against the Football League at Old Trafford and I had managed to mention to Matt Busby that I was not enjoying Italy and wanted to get back to Britain as soon as possible. Matt didn't say anything apart from muttering an expression of sympathy, and the conversation went no further.

The following April we met again when I was released to play for Scotland against England at Hampden. I deliberately went to the hotel where Matt was staying and had another word with him. I asked him if United would be interested should I become available. I did not expect him to say anything definite because that would have been unethical, but I told him that I was going to try and gain a release from my contract. Matt simply said that if I became available, then United would certainly make a bid. That was good enough for me.

It was April 1962 and when I returned to Italy I made it quite clear to the club that I had had enough of Italy and wanted to leave. I think they thought I was joking at first, or that I was throwing some sort of temperamental tantrum that they had seen countless times before from other players. I was quite resolved, though. I had spent a lot of time on my own while Joe Baker was recovering and it had not made me feel any better. As far as I was concerned I was already back in Britain.

We were playing in the quarter-final of the Italian Cup against Naples when I made what was to be my last appearance for Torino. The cup is not very high on the list of priorities in Italy. I suppose it had the same sort of status as our League Cup does now. In many ways it was a consolation prize, but it aggravated some of the bigger clubs who saw it as getting in the way of the more serious championship and European programmes. However, on 25 April 1962, there we were facing Napoli and just two games away from a place in the final. Only about 5,000 fans turned up to see the match, which gives some indication of the esteem in which the competition was held.

The strange thing I kept noticing during the game was that our manager, Beniamino Santos, was jumping up and down and getting very agitated. It was not like him. He was usually a calm, charming man for whom I had great personal regard. Most of his outbursts seemed to be aimed at me. I could not understand why, I was no better nor any worse than the rest of the side, but the more the game went on the more I realized that I was the exclusive subject of his apparent displeasure.

Eventually the referee called me over and I was sent off. I was stunned. I had not done anything wrong. After I left the pitch I became aware that my own manager had told the referee to order me from the field because I was not trying and was not listening to his instructions. I could not believe it. This was not the action of the man I had come to respect as my manager. It was obvious that he had received instructions from a higher authority. He could not look me in the eye. It seemed that Torino had taken my transfer request seriously after all and wanted to discredit me. By having me sent off it also meant that I would not be able to play for Scotland in the next scheduled international against Uruguay. They had not only managed to put the knife between my shoulder-blades but they had managed to twist it as well.

Napoli won 2–0 and after the game the Torino president, Angelo Fillipone, issued a statement which told everybody that I had given the impression I was saving myself for the international and that therefore I would be suspended for two weeks and I would not be made available for transfer. The president stated that both Law and Baker would be staying at the club.

That's what you think, pal!

While the rest of the squad went to Lausanne to play in a friendly tournament, I was left behind to brood. I was surprised, therefore, when I received a message to get on a train and join the others. This was indeed unexpected. One minute I was being punished and the next I was being asked to join the squad. The mystery was finally solved when I was informed that officials from Manchester United were also travelling to Lausanne, and that the reason for my journey was to discuss details of a transfer. I would have run all the way to Lausanne for that, let alone catch a train.

When I arrived in Lausanne, sure enough, Matt Busby was there along with several other officials of Manchester United. When asked if I would like to join the club I said 'yes' almost as quickly and emphatically as I did on the day that I was married. The deal was struck and I was told to return to Turin to pack my bags. I was on cloud nine as I sat on that train.

Yet there was a twist in the tale. The day after I returned to my apartment the club sent a car for me and I assumed that I was going to sign the necessary papers. Instead I was taken to the offices of Juventus. Here I found the Torino president and Umberto Agnelli, the president of Juventus, all smiles and handshakes. They cheerfully told me that Juventus had agreed to sign me and all I had to do was to put my signature on the piece of paper on Mr Agnelli's desk. Only two days earlier I had heard with my own ears a deal being struck between Torino and Manchester United for my transfer at a fee of £115,000. Now I was hearing that Juventus were prepared to pay £165,000 for me and, as a sweetener, I was to receive a signing-on fee of £12,000. I could not believe it until I remembered that I was still in Italy and that this was the Italian way of doing business.

I stated my case and said that there was not a snowball in hell's chance of me signing for Juventus as I was going back to Britain to play for Manchester United. They kept on talking. They pointed out that my contract with Juventus would make me a very rich man. Agnelli presented me with a gold watch and a gold tie-pin, which I told him to keep. He assured me that they were simply gifts and not inducements, but I did not want anything to do with what was going on and I refused them.

The charm gave way to threats and the shouting started. I was told that if I would not play for Juventus then I would not be playing for anybody. At the back of my mind I began to think about the prospects of playing in Australia since I did not think that a ban would apply there. I was determined to stick to my guns.

Eventually I was allowed to leave the office and let them continue talking. I went straight back to my apartment, scribbled a note for Joe Baker, who was training at the time, threw a few things into a bag, and called a taxi. To catch the next flight back to Britain I had to travel to Milan and I phoned ahead to some friends who booked me on the flight. Only a few hours later I was in London and catching another flight to Aberdeen.

When Torino heard that I had gone they were beside themselves with rage. Telegram after telegram rained down upon me in Aberdeen demanding my immediate return. I had been their top scorer that season and only four goals short of being the top scorer in the Italian League. They were not going to give up without a fight. But they could have sent those men in dark glasses and carrying violin-cases and I still would not have gone back. I had experienced enough of Italy. It was all over and nothing would have made me change my mind. I would sooner have worked on those Aberdeen trawlers.

6

UNITED AT LAST

Aberdeen was not just a haven for the fishing trawlers during the summer of 1962. It was also the retreat for yours truly. I had been successful in my escape from Italy but what was going to happen next was still a mystery. Torino kept sending me telegrams demanding my return, but there was no way I was going back there. I gambled that my ace card was the fact that Manchester United had put an offer of £115,000 on the table. If only I could hold out long enough for Torino to realize that, no matter how much they huffed and puffed, I would never change my mind. My gamble was that they would in the end grab the profit on the deal.

I tried to appear as relaxed as possible as I spent my time with the family, but the truth of the matter was that I was extremely agitated. I wanted to know where my career was taking me – that is, assuming I still had a career. The press boys gave me a call now and then but there was nothing I could tell them. The call that I was waiting for was from Manchester United to say that they had something for me to sign. The phone from that quarter remained silent, however.

You can imagine that every time the phone did ring I leaped up in the air. When it was a call from a reporter it always seemed a real anti-climax. Not that I minded them phoning, but I had nothing to tell them. The British press of those days was very different from the Italian. Here there was always a polite apology for disturbing you and a simple thank you when the conversation finished. If I had nothing to say, that was the end of it. Nobody tried to put words into my mouth. I regret that the British press these days has gone somewhat the way of the Italians. There are still a few good guys around, but there are also quite a few who have already written their story before they do the interview and get the facts.

So, I was reading a newspaper at home in Aberdeen when the phone rang yet again. I quickly dropped the paper and picked up the receiver. I was disappointed to find that it was Jim Rodgers, a reporter on the *Daily Record*. No disrespect to Jim but I had hoped it might have been someone with a Manchester accent. After a few words from Jim, however, I had completely changed my mind. If he had been in the room I would have kissed him as he told me the news. Torino had finally relented and had agreed to go ahead with the transfer of Denis Law to Manchester United. Gigi Peronace was already on his way to Manchester and I was expected to meet him there. Wow! I thanked Jim six or seven times, put the phone down and punched the air. Fantastic news!

I made a couple of calls just to make sure that no one had moved April Fool's day from April to July and, within an hour or two, I was on my way to Manchester. The actual signing was very civilized and quickly completed. I think that Torino must have had their fill of me, and Manchester United wanted to make sure that there would be no further complications. I signed my name faster than ever before or since. I shook hands with Gigi Peronace and he wished me all the best, which I appreciated since I had caused him problems from the first moment we had met. He had always looked beyond the problems, though, and knew that I had done my best for Torino. We parted with mutual respect and understanding.

At long last my future appeared to be settled and I was a Manchester United player. I had always had a feeling that one day I would join United. I know that is easy to say in hindsight, but even in my days at Maine Road it always seemed just a matter of time before I would be pulling on that famous red shirt at Old Trafford. I don't know if it was just wishful thinking on my part or whether I really did have a sixth sense about my eventual destiny. Probably it was the former. My encounters with Matt Busby had helped. After spending some time under the wing of Bill Shankly I knew that there was only going to be one other manager who would mean as much – if not more – to me, and that was Matt.

I could not wait to start pre-season training. Though the memories of Munich were still fresh and there was a rebuilding job going on, I felt that I had joined a club that was really high on ambition. Bobby Charlton was there of course, as were Harry Gregg, Bill Foulkes and a few others of the Munich era. Mostly, though, Manchester United was about new faces and up-and-coming youngsters, including an impish lad with an Ulster accent who was soon to become quite famous.

Busby was in the process of another rebuilding. The season before I joined United had finished in 15th place in what was then the First Division. It was not a vintage season even though the side had also reached the semi-finals of the FA Cup. The boss knew that there was quite a trek ahead before he could once again think in terms of Manchester United winning the European Cup, an ambition that burned both within himself and within the club.

By the time I started training, the excitement of joining United had evaporated a little. I was not happy about my high transfer fee, which was not of my choosing but which was being made a lot of by the media. What that achieved was the addition of more pressure – not just on myself but also on the club, who would come in for a lot of stick if the transfer did not work out too well. Anyway, there was no big thrill as the opening day of the season arrived, just a desire to get on with the job.

I can distinctly recall my first League match in a United shirt. We were at home to West Bromwich Albion on the first day of the season, a warm afternoon in August 1962. There was no

Bobby Charlton in the side because he was still recovering from a hernia operation, but the atmosphere was nevertheless one of great expectation, as indeed it always has been at Old Trafford from decades ago right up to the present day.

I did not feel particularly nervous as we ran out on to the pitch but I will always remember the roar that met the team as we emerged from the tunnel. It was a roar that I was to hear so often and yet never take for granted. I wanted to do well of course and, when David Herd scored after just five minutes, I felt we were on the way to success. Two minutes later a great cross from Johnny Giles was perfectly placed for me and I headed the ball into the net to make it 2–0. I was thrilled to bits by that and raised my arm in salute to the fans. Someone took a photo of that and it was so well used in the newspapers that it became a kind of trade-mark. I did not do it on purpose every time I scored, it was just an instinctive reaction. Today I hear about players planning and rehearsing their celebration routines. It makes me shake my head in disbelief at times.

The scene was set for an opening-day victory but West Bromwich fought back and scored twice to make the final score 2–2. On reflection it was probably a fair result, but not the one I wanted. Just four days later there was our first away game, another League match, this time at Everton. The previous season United had been beaten 1–5 at Everton, so it is possible, years later, to say that our 1–3 defeat was almost an improvement. Of course, anyone saying such a thing at the time would have been subjected to the wrath of Law. I was very disappointed.

Three days after the Everton defeat we were away again. Our journey took us to London this time, to Highbury, which might at one time have become my home ground. On the opposition side should have been my old pal Joe Baker. He had left Torino shortly after me and was now a member of what was a good Arsenal side. He missed that game because of an injury but he and I still managed to have a chat after the match. At last the side clicked as we knew we could and, even though we were still unable to field our strongest team, we won 3–1. As I trooped off the field with the others I realized that this was my first competitive victory in a United shirt, and one that I should definitely commit to memory.

I wish that the return with Everton a few days later had been equally as memorable. As it was, we lost 0–1 at home and after just four games one of our rivals had already done the double over us. Bad news! Our erratic form meant that we then beat Birmingham 2–0 at home before losing 0–3 at Bolton. This was not quite the way the season had been planned and what was worse for me personally was that I had not scored since the opening day. Surely that would change when we travelled down to London again? This time we were to meet Leyton Orient, who were experiencing their first season – and only one so far – in the First Division. They had not got off to a good start, but their fans had a real East London knees-up after they beat us 1–0 with a late goal from their winger Terry McDonald.

Back at Old Trafford we beat Bolton 3–0, which restored some of our self-confidence and set us up for our first really big match of the season – a home clash against Manchester City. Yes, it was my first derby game in a United shirt. It was one of those good-news, bad-news jobs, so I'll give you the good news first. I scored twice against my old club, which was very satisfying because it ended my goal drought and also put one over on City. The bad news was that they scored three.

I scored two in the following match as well, but once again we were beaten at home. This time it was Burnley who inflicted the damage and hammered five goals past us. In the next four games we drew one and lost three, including getting a 2–6 thumping at Tottenham. Even the return of Bobby Charlton to the side did not seem to change things very much. Here we were with a third of the season gone and only three victories and two drawn games in the 14 that we had played. We were already looking up at most of our rivals and, while nobody dared mention the word 'crisis', we knew that things weren't going exactly as we had all hoped.

Our policy at that time was to make sure that we scored lots of goals. It did not matter how many the opposition scored as long as we scored more than them. Unfortunately, most of our opponents had not been let in on the secret and therefore spoiled things, either by defending too well or by scoring more goals than we did. Ipswich, though, were very cooperative. We had just ended our bad run by beating West Ham 3–1 at home when we played away to Ipswich, who happened to be the reigning champions. I could not put a foot wrong that day and, while the home team put three past us, we scored five, of which my own personal tally was four. Another game for the memory bank.

We were on a bit of a roll now as we drew with Liverpool 3–3, beat Wolves 3–2, drew our next two games, and then beat Nottingham Forest 5–1. That last-mentioned game was on 8 December 1962, and before my next football match I was to become a changed person. Something happened to me that has had a profound effect on my life up to the present day. I got married to Di.

We had met at a dance-hall – where else? – during my sojourn in Aberdeen and began a whirlwind romance that is still whirling. She was not impressed by the fact that I was a professional footballer – and that impressed me. It was good to be able to talk about a host of other things without football coming into the conversation. We had not known each other for very long when I popped the question. She had told me that she worked in a solicitor's office. I had to make her name Law after that, didn't I? We used to see quite a bit of each other even though we were hundreds of miles apart. British Airways must have made a fortune out of our trips but so far they have never even sent us a wedding anniversary card. Now that's what I call mean!

Matt Busby was delighted when he heard that I was getting married. He liked his players to have settled private lives and, as a Scotsman, he could think of nobody better to marry than a Scottish girl.

On Tuesday 11 December 1962 Diana Rosemary Leith Thomson became my Lawful wedded wife and I have never regretted it for one moment. We have had a great marriage and we are the best of friends – something of which I am very proud.

We had the briefest of honeymoons because the following Saturday we – the team that is – were away to West Bromwich Albion as we began the second half of the season. We were beaten 0–3 but I promise it had nothing to do with my honeymoon – honest!

That West Bromwich game was another that I remember quite vividly for a very strange reason. Like most professional players I was well used to being heckled and abused by spectators, but it came as a bit of a shock when it was the referee who started on me. His name was Gilbert Pullin and he was definitely not a member of the Denis Law fan club. Throughout the first half he continually made rude comments every time I missed a shot or failed in some other way. I had a chat with the boss at half-time and he told me to do my best to ignore it. I believe that Matt thought the referee would give it a rest in the second half. He didn't. At the end of the game Matt and I decided that we should put in a complaint to the Football Association.

The upshot of a disciplinary hearing was that Mr Pullin was censured and he became so upset by this that he quit. I felt sorry for him. I had wanted some sort of action but it had all gone a lot further than I had expected. The ripples from dropping that pebble in the pond stayed with me for the rest of my career. There is a strong sense of brotherhood among referees and from that moment on I was a marked man. I was rarely given the benefit of any doubt and I often found myself in trouble for retaliation after I had been kicked all over the park by an opponent who escaped unpenalized.

As it happened, there was plenty of time for Di and I to get used to being married because the snow fell so heavily as we beat Fulham 1–0 on Boxing Day that we did not have another first-team match for almost two months. The big freeze of the 1962–63 season took its toll and football had to take an enforced mid-campaign break. We were living in a club house which was not exactly the height of luxury. There were no carpets, which meant that the floor was always freezing cold. We were not very well off for furniture either and central heating and double glazing were things of the future. The result was that Di and I found ourselves living in something which reminded us both of the cold storage warehouses back in Aberdeen. After that start it's no wonder that our marriage has survived so well.

During the big freeze Matt went into the transfer market once again and bought a player who turned out to be one of his most important signings. I'm talking about Pat Crerand, who joined in February 1963 from Celtic. Matt had two players in mind because he was also thinking of signing Jim Baxter from Rangers. I was flattered when he not only asked my opinion but also acted upon it. Matt was not going to buy both players and he asked me which of the two I thought would be most useful to Manchester United. I told him that, as an individual, Jim Baxter was the more skilful and probably the more entertaining too, but if he wanted someone who would fit in, quietly get on with the job and in the long term be a better investment, then he should go for Pat Crerand.

The boss puffed on his pipe as he listened and the next thing I knew was that on 6 February 1963, significantly a day when Manchester was remembering the Munich disaster of exactly five years earlier, Pat Crerand signed on the dotted line and became another Scot at Old Trafford. I think the years that followed proved what a wise choice he was and I am glad to have been a part of it.

Once the thaw started and the pitches became playable again we set about recapturing the run we had put together during the seven matches prior to my wedding. Our first game back was a Division One encounter at home to Blackpool. They were a tough side to beat in those days and it was no disgrace to end up with a draw. Another draw was the result of our next match away to Blackburn, following which we went on the FA Cup trail. It was about two months late but nevertheless welcome since it meant that we would be playing against one of my old clubs again. We had been drawn at home to Huddersfield. Naturally I wanted to have a good performance and a great result against Huddersfield and I certainly was not disappointed. We beat them 5–0 and I got a hat-trick which was extremely gratifying.

The Football Association and the Football League were going crazy to try and get all the fixtures played because of the huge backlog caused by the weather. They could not delay the end of the season indefinitely or else we would have finished up playing throughout the summer. We played three FA Cup rounds in as many weeks and, having started our campaign at the beginning of March, we had reached the semi-final by the end of it. In those few weeks we knocked out Aston Villa, Chelsea and Coventry without any replays and we were starting to look good for a place in the final itself.

Our League form was a different matter. Having started back with those two drawn games we then suffered four successive defeats, three of them at Old Trafford. If it had not been for our Cup run I think that the clouds over our part of Manchester would have been too heavy to bear. As it was we had a fight on our hands and the confidence we gained from our Cup games served to remind us that we were a quality side with no business being at the bottom of the table.

Because of the fixture backlog we were playing crucial matches every few days. I think it became more a matter of who would crack first under the pressure than on which teams were the best or worst. By the end of April we were still in a very dangerous position but we had a respite of a few days from our League worries as we had a date with Southampton at Villa Park for the FA Cup semi-final. In the other tie Liverpool and Leicester were doing battle. We felt that we had been given the better deal by being drawn against

Southampton. No disrespect to the Saints but they were a Second Division side at that time, so surely we couldn't be blamed for fancying our chances of reaching Wembley.

As often seems to be the case, our semi-final against Southampton was not much of a spectacle for the spectators. Nobody wants to give anything away in a semi-final and that usually produces dour games in which both sides are intent only in getting a result. How they get it is of no concern. Entertaining the fans is the last thing on any manager's mind. He just wants to get his team to the final.

I'm glad I didn't have to pay to watch the match. There was just one goal and I got rave reviews for scoring it. Personally I thought it was a very scrappy effort that barely deserved to go in but, if the newspapers wanted to refer to me as a hero, who was I to complain? They said that I had showed quick thinking, courage and skill. What actually happened was that I miskicked the ball, but it wedged under my leg as I fell over and I had a second chance at prodding it home. Since the Southampton goalkeeper, Ron Reynolds, and his defenders had committed themselves for my first attempt, they were helpless as the ball rolled into the net.

Southampton tried hard to equalize and went close several times, but in the end that single goal was enough to see us through. Leicester won the other semi-final and we had the great prospect of ending our season with a part to play in the most famous Cup Final in world football.

However, there was still the very serious matter of avoiding relegation. With just ten days of the League season left we had four games still to play and each one was going to be crucial. Leyton Orient were already relegated, but who was to join them? It could be Birmingham City, Manchester City, or ourselves. The first of our remaining fixtures was away to Birmingham. They guaranteed their safety by beating us 2–1. I scored our goal but it was no consolation. The only good thing was that our rivals at Maine Road were on the wrong end of their scoreline and, since their record for the season was worse than ours, the pressure on them was even greater. That was some consolation, especially as they were to be our next opponents.

We travelled the short distance to Maine Road knowing that a draw would be of greater value to us than to City. They had to win to put the pressure on us. Fairly early on City went ahead through Alex Harley and they were throwing the kitchen sink at us. Matt told us to keep calm and keep plugging away and we would be all right. We did just that and eventually Matt's words came true. I chased after a loose ball in the area and the City goalkeeper, Harry Dowd, wrestled me to the ground. It was a moment of madness by Harry because there was no real chance of me getting the ball. We were grateful for the penalty, though most of us hoped that it would not be our job to take it. No worry about that. Albert Quixall stepped up as bold as brass and, while the majority of his team-mates had their backs to him and were offering up prayers, he calmly side-footed the ball into the net.

We came away with a point that we probably did not deserve, but the pressure was greatly relieved. We had two matches still to play and one of them was at home to Leyton Orient. On the same day, the last of the League season, City were away to West Ham, so it was a clash between East London and Manchester.

There was a scare for us when Orient surprisingly took the lead, but an own goal and one each from Bobby Charlton and yours truly gave us a 3–1 win. The really good news came when we left the pitch because we then learned that West Ham had done us proud. They thrashed City 6–1 and that was definitely the end of the relegation battle. We were safe. Several of us were rested for the last League match of the season, which ended in a 1–2 defeat at Nottingham Forest. It was meaningless. We finished in 19th place and resolved that we did not want that kind of scare again.

My first season at Old Trafford was drawing to a close and it had been quite an experience. I had learned a few things, not least to listen to Matt Busby. He had tried to curb my impatience. I always wanted to be involved in the game all of the time – so much so that I sometimes used to run back deep into our own half and take the ball from the feet of my team-mates. Matt stopped that and made me wait my turn. At one stage he virtually banned me from going back into our own half at all. He told me to concentrate on scoring and he was right. At the end of our League programme I had scored 23 goals in 38 games and that put me at the top of our list, four goals more than David Herd. Between us we had claimed 42 of our 67 goals.

Could we keep up the scoring in the FA Cup Final? That was the jackpot question. Even more interesting was the fact that, in terms of form, we were actually the underdogs – a rare role for Manchester United.

The big day was soon upon us. Leicester had been pipped for the championship by Everton and were keen not to let another trophy slip through their fingers. I'm sure that the days leading up to Wembley were more traumatic for them than for us. We had a relaxed approach because we had nothing to lose since Leicester were such hot favourites. We trained and spent time together and I think it was quite noticeable that there were smiles on our faces in the tunnel before the game, while our opponents seemed quite uptight.

It is a unique experience playing in the FA Cup Final, and I must say that our coach trip to the great stadium was marvellous. As you get near to Wembley you take in the great atmosphere. You see the opposition supporters of course, but you also see throngs of your own fans and it gives you a lift. You recognize many of the faces and soon realize you are among friends. There were a lot of laughs on our coach and we were in party mood throughout the hours before the kick-off.

My wife, Di, was in the stadium and I could see her sitting with the other players' wives and girlfriends. We were all waving to them as we walked out alongside our opponents and drank in the experience of hearing those 100,000 voices ringing around that mighty stadium.

The Manchester United team on that sunny afternoon of 25 May 1963 was: David Gaskell in goal, Tony Dunne, Pat Crerand, Bill Foulkes, Maurice Setters, Johnny Giles, Albert Quixall, David Herd, Bobby Charlton, our captain, Noel Cantwell and yours truly.

Anyone who saw the game will, I hope, agree that it was a great performance. The fact that we had several players capable of using the wide open spaces of the Wembley pitch gave us a distinct advantage and we played the sort of football that we had been promising all season. I think the new Manchester United arrived on that day.

The match had been going for just a quarter of an hour when Pat Crerand found me with a terrific pass. I whacked the ball past Gordon Banks from close range and a sea of red on the terraces leaped into the air. We were in the lead. Leicester fought back but they were very regimented. Their manager, Matt Gillies, later admitted that their precision probably cost them the game. You have to be able to improvise and adapt at Wembley, allowing players to utilize their individual skills. Matt Busby had given us the freedom to express ourselves and we took full advantage.

David Herd scored a second for us just after half-time and we were on our way to victory. Leicester did not give up, though, and pulled a goal back through Keyworth. We did not panic but simply kept on playing a passing game. A cross came over and I met it with my head. The ball thudded against the woodwork and rebounded. I jumped again in the hope of a second chance and Gordon Banks followed me. That left the way open for David Herd to meet the ball and slam it into the net. Now we were 3–1 ahead and we kept it that way.

After receiving the trophy and parading it around the stadium, I had the joy of a reunion with my wife and a celebration banquet. I clutched my medal from the moment I received it to the time I went to sleep. It was the first medal that I had ever won as a professional footballer and was a great souvenir of a dream day.

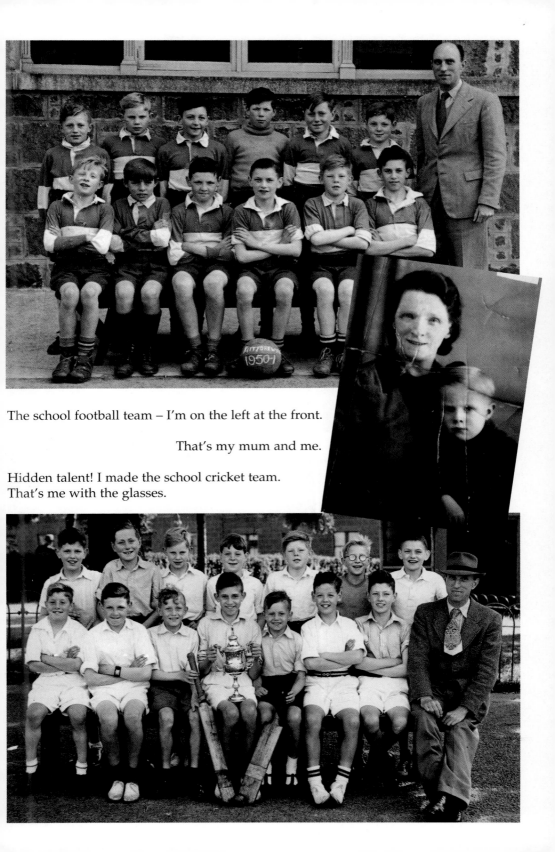

The school football team – I'm on the left at the front.

That's my mum and me.

Hidden talent! I made the school cricket team.
That's me with the glasses.

This is when I posed for a cigarette card at Huddersfield. Not really!

Manchester City days. Note the modern boots.

(©Colorsport)

Signing for City the first time.

Myself, Gerry Hitchens and Joe Baker prepare to play for the Italian League.

The moment I became a Manchester United player.

The FA Cup win of 1963, dressing room celebrities with Noel, Pat and Bobby.

What a wedding – even the cake was in tiers.

Receiving the European Footballer of the Year Award, 1964.

(©Colorsport)

Stopped by Banks and Moore, two all-time greats.

I just had to swap with Bobby Charlton after that 1967 game.

(©Colorsport)

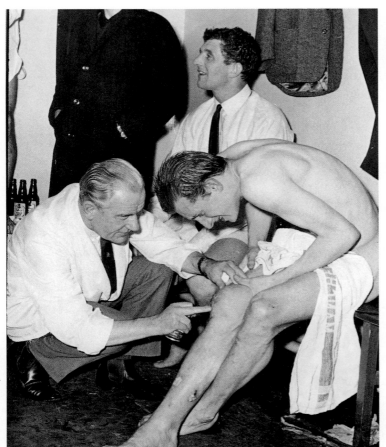

(Manchester Daily Mail)

Showing off my latest war wound – but this was a bad one.

ABOVE RIGHT: Hey, look at this, it's the Championship.

BELOW RIGHT: Parading with the boss after winning the title in 1967.

Yippee! Another goal from the Lawman.

(©Colorsport)

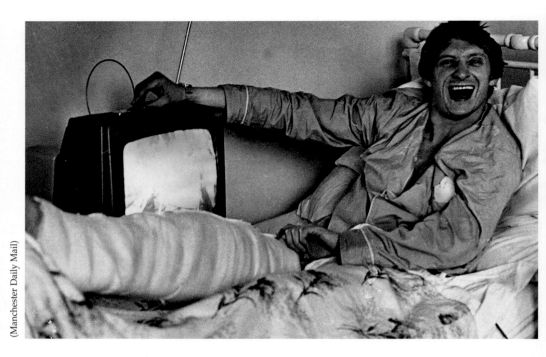

(Manchester Daily Mail)

We've won the European Cup – I wake up the other patients.

The squad that conquered Europe.

(©Colorsport)

When I had joined Manchester United a year earlier, part of my decision was based on the ambition that made the club so vibrant. Our League form had been disappointing, to say the least. All that was now forgotten as the name of Manchester United was engraved on the trophy. We had given notice that we could play as well as anyone – and better than most.

The slumbering giant of Old Trafford had awakened.

7

OLD TRAFFORD MAGIC

The summer of 1963 was certainly a change from the previous one. I did not have to go into hiding in Aberdeen. After we returned from Wembley and the after-match banquet, we went on a special tour from Central Station to Manchester Town Hall. An open-top bus had been arranged so that we could parade the FA Cup and let all our supporters see it. I think that most of Manchester turned out on that night. It was fantastic. Manchester had been waiting for something to celebrate since Munich and, at last, they were able to let their hair down. I was amazed that on the route a huge red and white arch of triumph had been erected. We only travelled a mile but it took us nearly an hour. It was a reception that I shall always remember.

There was a bit of uncertainty hanging over us, though, because we had been promised a bonus, but did not know exactly what we were to receive. We did know that Burnley's players had each got £1,000 for their appearance in the previous year's final – and they had been the losers. We had also heard that Leicester's players had been offered a similar amount if they won. Newspaper speculation had led us to believe that our bonus would be in the region of £2,000 per man. You know what they say about not counting your chickens before they are hatched.

At the end of the season we went on a short tour of Italy, ironically playing our first game against Juventus in my less-than-happy hunting ground of Turin. We had been in Italy just a few days when the boss told us that our bonus for winning the FA Cup would be £20 each. There was a stunned silence. We all thought it was a joke at first but quickly realized that Matt was perfectly serious. Our silence gave way to anger and several players went to see Matt. He explained that the club chairman, Mr Hardman, had been loath to go to the board for a bonus fund for winning the FA Cup when our League season had been less than spectacular. I think that everyone concerned was highly embarrassed and the whole matter was swept swiftly under the carpet. We felt aggrieved, but there was nothing we could do about it and so we put it down to experience.

I did have one bonus that summer, though, when I had the great privilege of captaining Scotland for two games on our summer tour. We lost 0–1 to the Republic of Ireland in Dublin, but we beat Spain 6–2 in Madrid. After that Di and I had a holiday and by the time I had to report back for training for the 1963–64 season I was in the right frame of mind to play my part in United's assault on the championship.

Johnny Giles left us for Leeds during the summer but, as the new season dawned, one of the greatest names in the game was on the eve of stardom. I'm speaking, of course, about George Best.

We had to play Everton in the FA Charity Shield and any thoughts we might have had about conquering all before us were soon swept away when they gave us a 4–0 roasting. It taught us a sharp lesson and we were determined that we would not allow that sort of thing to happen again when the serious business of the League began.

Our first fixture was a visit to Hillsborough and we came away with a 3–3 draw. That was an improvement on our trip there of the previous season when we had lost 0–1, and Wednesday had also beaten us at Old Trafford, so we were not too displeased with our draw on the opening day of the season. A few days later we beat Ipswich at home 2–0 and I scored my first goals of the new campaign.

The first major test came on the second Saturday when we were at home to Everton, the reigning champions and, of course, victors over us in the Charity Shield. There were over 63,000 inside Old Trafford for the game, and a few thousand more locked outside. We had a horror start when Tony Dunne deflected the ball past Harry Gregg to give our opponents the lead. I should think that the crowd still waiting outside could hear what Harry had to say about that. Harry and I were often room-mates. What a character! A superb goalkeeper with an enormous personality. I used to call him 'Brillo-Head' because of his wiry hair, and he called me all kinds of things in return. Many a young player had his vocabulary greatly enlarged by listening to Harry.

Everton were ahead after eight minutes but it served only to sting us into greater effort. Or perhaps it was Harry Gregg's stinging remarks! We drew level and then went on the rampage. When we were 4–1 ahead I asked the supporters if they wanted more. They did. I scored my second goal of the game and they were happy at 5–1, which gave us the same four-goal margin by which we had been beaten in the Charity Shield. At the end of that game it was party time. I'm not sure which was the noisier, the crowd on the terraces or the team in the dressing room.

We were still in that same frame of mind when we travelled to Portman Road a few days later for our return match with Ipswich. The previous season I had scored four goals as we beat them 5–3. I wasn't expecting to repeat that but I was certainly prepared to give it my best shot. As it happened I was restricted to a hat-trick but, while I was getting a fair bit of close attention, the others popped in four more goals to give us a 7–2 victory.

After a 1–1 draw at Birmingham we had home victories over West Bromwich and Blackpool and were at the top of the table. The win over West Bromwich was particularly significant because it marked the first-team début of George Best. Manchester United would never be the same again. It was all going exactly as we had hoped and planned – that is until we suffered successive defeats at Arsenal and Blackpool. We suddenly awoke to the fact that we might not be invincible after all.

Our European Cup Winners' Cup campaign began well. We were drawn against Willem II and, after a 1–1 draw in Holland, we beat them 6–1 at Old Trafford and comfortably qualified for the next round.

After our hiccups against Blackpool and Arsenal we pulled ourselves together again and won three of our next four games – an away draw at Chelsea being the only point dropped. Things were looking up again and I had one of the greatest thrills of my life when I was selected to play for a Rest of the World side against England at Wembley in a centenary game for the FA. The team in which I was to play was full of stars, players like Di Stefano, Masopust, Djalma Santos, Kopa, Yashin, Seeler, Eyzaguirre, and my Scotland pal Jim Baxter. The only disappointment was that Pelé was unable to play because of injury.

As I sat in the dressing room before the match on 23 October 1963, it was like a dream. For the first time in my life I was completely awestruck. The world's most famous footballers, every one of them a legend in his own right, were pulling on the same shirt as me. The game itself was a bit disjointed. The England players took it all very seriously and were interested only in winning. The Rest of the World side wanted to put on a show that would live for ever in the memories of that Wembley crowd.

England scored twice and beat us 2–1. Our goal was a hell of a consolation for me, though. I saw Puskas break through the middle with the ball glued to his feet. He went about 40 yards, saw me in a space and presented me with a perfect opportunity to slip the ball past Gordon Banks in the England goal. It was a moment that I have always cherished and, despite all my wonderful experiences with United and other clubs and Scotland too, scoring that goal was probably the highlight of my career. For night after night afterwards I went to sleep reliving the experience.

A few weeks later that dream made way for a nightmare. I scored a hat-trick in our 4–1 win over Tottenham at Old Trafford, but the following week we were on the receiving end of a 4–0 thumping by Aston Villa. For me it was not just the defeat but the fact that I was sent off in an incident that I still believe was a grave injustice to me.

I had become a prime target for defenders and it was a rare game in which I was not kicked from one side of the pitch to the other. Other goal-scorers had the same treatment – they still do. My problem was that I too easily took the law into my own hands and I had been cautioned a few times prior to our match with Villa. In that game I was taking more than the usual stick from Alan Deakin and some time in the second half, when I was clattered for the umpteenth time by him, I gestured retaliation. I never touched him but the referee pointed instantly towards the dressing room. I could hardly believe it, but there was no mistake. I trudged off angrily. Many players have experienced the same thing. The referee offers no protection, and if you do not protect yourself you realize there's a good chance that you may end up in hospital. You are cut and bruised and have your legs raked or worse but, the moment you threaten retribution, you are the one in trouble while your attacker gets away without so much as a talking-to.

My sending-off that day at Villa Park was followed by a further injustice when I was subsequently banned for 28 days, which was a very severe sentence at that time.

Just before my suspension began we played Stoke and I scored four goals as we won 5–2. It was small consolation as I had to sit out the next four League matches and the second leg of our European Cup Winners' Cup second-round game against Tottenham, who had beaten us 2–0 in the first leg.

During my absence we had two bad away defeats. We lost 0–4 at Everton and 1–6 at Burnley on Boxing Day. Two days later we were avenged when United beat Burnley in the home fixture 5–1. The return leg of the European Cup Winners' Cup was particularly agonizing. Trailing 0–2 from the first leg, we really needed to be at full strength for the return. As I watched, my Scotland team-mate, Dave McKay, broke his leg. It was a sickening blow because he was such a great player. I could see the tackle coming and I actually yelled for it not to happen. But it did, and there was a loud crack and within minutes Iron Man Dave was on his way to hospital. We won 4–1 and that put us into the third round on a 4–3 aggregate.

I could not wait to get back into action but it was mid-January 1964 before I returned. There were some exciting moments during the rest of the season but I think that losing twice to Liverpool was what sealed our fate. We had lost to them at home and then they beat us 3–0 at Anfield. Since they ended the season as champions and we were runners-up just four points behind, the significance of those two defeats could hardly have been more apparent.

Once again inconsistency let us down in our bid for the championship that season, but, in finishing second, we had certainly made quite a few people eat their words and our own self-belief was not at all harmed. In addition to being runners-up in the championship, we reached the semi-finals of the FA Cup. Having disposed of Southampton, Bristol Rovers and Barnsley, we were drawn against Sunderland in the sixth round, and what an epic that turned out to be. They held us to a 3–3 draw at Old Trafford and then we had to go to extra-time at Roker Park in the replay before the game ended at 2–2. The second replay was held at Huddersfield and I think that Sunderland had run out of steam by then because they were not the same team that had given us such a hard time in the previous two matches. I had sufficient space to score a hat-trick and we beat them 5–1.

We had only to beat West Ham to be back at Wembley for a second successive season. It always makes me laugh to hear commentators say, 'He had *only* the goalkeeper to beat', or 'They had *only* to beat so-and-so to clinch the title.' I often wish that the tables could be turned and players could say things like, 'He had *only* to talk into the microphone to get my name right.' Do you get my point?

Anyway, we *only* had to beat West Ham and, after all, they *only* had players like Bobby Moore and Geoff Hurst in their side. We met at Hillsborough and they won 3–1. I scored our goal but it was not enough and, as the history books record, the Hammers went on to Wembley where they beat Preston 3–2.

After our exit from the FA Cup we were back in European Cup Winners' Cup action a few days later. It was the third round and we were playing Sporting Lisbon. Victory would put us into the semi-finals. However, once again we were in a difficult situation because of a fixture pile-up. Our FA Cup semi-final against West Ham had been our fifth high-profile game in 15 days and we had just four days to prepare and travel to Portugal for our second-leg tie against Sporting Lisbon.

We had roasted them at Old Trafford and won 4–1. I scored my second hat-trick of that season's European Cup Winners' Cup and, despite our flagging energy, we did not think we would have too much trouble in getting through to the semi-finals. That was nearly confirmed after the first few minutes of the game when I hit the woodwork. However, that seemed to make our hosts realize that they were on a hiding to nothing and they changed from the over-defensive side which had visited Old Trafford into an attacking band of dervishes. We were stunned as they scored goal after goal to cancel out our advantage, and then went ahead. The final score was 5–0, and 6–4 on aggregate. Sporting went on to win the trophy that season.

It was disappointing to have been so near and yet so far in those three major competitions. There was some consolation in that our youth side, including George Best, won the FA Youth Cup, because that meant that the future of Manchester United was looking good. There was also some joy in the news that Old Trafford had been selected to be among the venues for the

1966 World Cup – and that set me thinking. As a Scotsman I was never likely to have the pleasure of playing in a World Cup tournament on my home ground. Making it to the 1966 World Cup tournament was the next best thing, especially if, by some fluke, Scotland was drawn in a group which was to play at Old Trafford. The prospect of that was exciting, to say the least.

The other good things to come out of that season were the débuts of David Sadler and George Best. David had been promoted from the youth team and had no problem in finding his feet in the first team. George, of course, was George. He drove defenders crazy and more than a few seemed to be after his blood from the moment he first joined the senior team.

I have to admit that I was not too sure of him at first. Oh yes, he had talent all right, an abundance of it, but I had heard about him fleeing Manchester because he was homesick and I wondered if he had the temperament to see it through. We all knew what it was like to miss the folks back home but getting over all that is a part of the growing up process. It worried me that George was prepared to give in to it so easily. (Looking back, though, I don't think there ever needed to be any real concern about the homesickness. I don't believe that those early scarpers that George performed were in any way related to the disappearing acts later on in his career.)

Another concern was the fact that he was so slight. He almost had to run around in the shower to get wet. I thought he might be knocked off the ball too easily. As it happened I had no need to worry about that; he never stood still long enough for a defender to get close to him. He was magnificent and I warmed to him as soon as we were team-mates. Yes, he used to give me some verbal stick during the game, but then I gave him some back and what is said during a match does not reflect the true relationship. In the heat of the moment, with about 50,000 people yelling at you, you are not quite your normal calm self.

In George Best Manchester United had unearthed an

absolute diamond. There was no question that he was one of the best, if not *the* best, player of his type that Britain has ever produced. I have seen grown men almost in tears after tackling what turned out to be thin air only to see him already yards away racing down the touchline with the ball. He knew he was good too and had absolute confidence in himself. He loved to beat players and make them look stupid. He used to drive us mad sometimes. He would often get the ball, beat two or three players and then wait for them to catch up so that he could beat them again. Meanwhile we were screaming at him to release the ball to one of us so that we could get on with the job of scoring goals. He just used to grin at us. I could have thumped him many a time, but how could you discourage such incredible skill, talent and personality?

I had been with an agent for some time and I introduced George to him. Ken Stanley was the man, and it was Ken who played a major part in making George such a big star. In those days agents simply looked after your activities away from football. They would take care of your media work – opening shops, advertising baked beans or anything else that was producing extra income – but they did not involve themselves in your transfers or contracts. That was nothing to do with them and they kept well clear of it.

Ken Stanley was very good at his work. He helped me a great deal and of course he helped George as well. During the following years you could hardly move without seeing George grinning at you from a magazine cover, a huge advertisement on a wall, from bedspreads, coat-hangers, posters, T-shirts and so on. You name it, George had his face on it. Ken Stanley realized from the start that George was not only a great footballer but a good-looking lad with loads of charisma. He could not fail – and he didn't.

The 1963–64 season ended with us as the bridesmaids. For me personally it had not been a bad season, apart from the suspension. I had scored 30 goals in 30 League matches, ten goals in six FA Cup ties, and six goals in five European Cup

Winners' Cup matches. I had played for the Rest of the World and continued my Scotland career. I could not really complain too much about not picking up any medals that season. By finishing second we had qualified for the Inter-Cities Fairs Cup, which meant that we would be having another crack at Europe.

I reflected that I was now at the end of my ninth season as a professional footballer and my second at United. I had one FA Cup winners' medal to show for it and I dearly wanted to win a championship medal. Perhaps my tenth season would also make it third time lucky with United. It was going to be an eventful summer break, but little did I know that it was going to be followed by an equally eventful 1964–65 season.

8

CHAMPIONS

The dust soon settled on the season, but for Di and myself there was no quick dash on to a plane to Spain or Malta. We took a car to hospital instead. Two of us were in the car going there, and three of us made the return journey as Gary, our first son, was born on 21 June 1964. He was worth far more than all the medals and awards put together and I have always taken far more pleasure and pride in my family than in any of my football achievements.

So I was a pretty happy guy when I reported back for pre-season training at Old Trafford. We had a new face in the squad because John Connelly had joined us from Burnley. We knew John only too well since he had always put in such great performances against us, and it was a real pleasure to welcome him to Manchester United as one of our own. I felt that it was a very wise signing by Matt because we needed someone who was a definite right-winger. Different players had been used in that position but John Connelly was a specialist.

Before the season proper began, we played a friendly against Hamburg in Germany and Connelly scored twice. As we travelled back home I began mulling over our prospects for the season. I know it is very easy to be wise after an event but it did occur to me at that time that we had a perfect squad for taking the championship. As I considered all the different departments I could not see a single flaw. We also had great team spirit and the ability to work well as a unit. I could hardly wait for the start of the 1964–65 season.

We began with a home match against West Bromwich Albion in front of the usual huge Old Trafford crowd. Warming up in front of the Stretford Enders was like meeting up with all your mates again. The season did not start as well as we had hoped because West Brom took the lead fairly early on. Not long afterwards, though, John Connelly sent over a perfect cross from the right. I leaped in the air and headed it home and then saluted the supporters. We were on our way. The game ended at 2–2 but we were not unhappy with that. The first day of the season always throws up some rogue results when you compare them later with the way the season goes.

We were less than happy after our next two games, though. West Ham beat us 3–1. Once again we lost an early goal and this time we did not fight back as well and we were 0–2 down before I scored what was to be our consolation goal. I scored again in our next game, away to Leicester, hitting our equaliser two minutes before the end. The scoreline was 2–2 but the headline was rather different.

The game had been only two minutes old when I collided with the referee, a gentleman called Wells. It was a complete accident. I was following the ball and didn't see him trying to get out of the way. There was a bit of a crunch and, while I took some of the impact, he took the worst of it. The poor chap was on the ground for some time receiving attention before he could continue, but he did shake hands afterwards and there were no hard feelings – except for the bruises which, no doubt, he carried for some days after.

That was an unfortunate and accidental clash with a referee which we both regretted. I had another clash with a different referee some weeks later. I regretted it, but by his own admission, he made money out of it, which I found distasteful to say the least.

My first encounter with this man could not have come at a worse time because the Football Association was making a big deal about discipline and had even threatened suspension of half a season for offenders.

It often amazes me how much things have changed. The hard tackles of my day are now exaggerated by the dramatics of players writhing in agony as if they have just had a three-hour session with the Spanish Inquisition. You only saw that sort of thing in Italy when I was playing. If someone came in hard on you there were two options. You either kept out of his way for the rest of the game or you repaid the compliment. Nowadays you see the most amazing antics. While one player is enacting the death scene from *Antony and Cleopatra*, his mates jostle the referee demanding that he produce a card, preferably a red one. I have seen players in a threatening stance, aggressively using the worst possible language at referees and simply being waved away. If any player did that in my day he would have been sent off, hauled before the FA, fined and suspended for some weeks.

Well, when I encountered this referee, I was having a run-in with Alan Ball. He had obviously been told to mark me out of the game and you could never accuse Bally of shirking his responsibilities. I did not appreciate his attention being as close as it was and so I did what I always did – gave him some stick in return. Perhaps I was a little over-zealous, I don't know. Anyway, I was booked for a foul. The lumps kicked out of my own shins mattered not a jot to the man in charge. And it got worse.

Paddy Crerand ran over and told me to calm down. I didn't need that kind of advice and I told him so in a way that I knew he would understand – shall we say 'colourfully'? The next thing I knew was that I was being sent off. Anybody with half a brain would have known I was talking to Paddy, but the referee chose to believe that my expletive-laden response to Paddy was actually directed at himself.

Of course the media became very excited and our 2–1 victory was overshadowed by the speculation about whether yours truly was to be suspended for months. I asked for a personal hearing and was granted one, at which Paddy gave evidence of the circumstances. The FA were not impressed and I was fined £50 and banned for 28 days, which meant that I would receive no pay and would miss the Christmas matches. I did not mind spending Christmas in Aberdeen but it was frustrating to think of the reason why I was there.

That was still not the end of the matter because my team-mates decided to have a whip-round to provide me with a bit of cash while I was not earning. Remember that this was in the days when top earners were just about into three figures and not the five-figure sums that are earned today. The newspapers picked up on the story and it was not long before the FA stepped in and said they would take a dim view of any such action as it would undermine their authority to enforce discipline. I did not want to be the cause of any further trouble and so it was agreed that the idea, although well appreciated by me, would be dropped.

Even that was not the end of the affair. Everything that happens at a private hearing at the Football Association is always held to be strictly confidential. Somehow a Sunday paper got the full SP on what had happened. I was amazed. I had refused to discuss it with any journalist. The FA launched an investigation and discovered that the 'mole' had been the referee. He was ordered not to do such a thing again.

I suppose you must think that that must surely be the end of it? Wrong! Some years later I was at Barcelona airport with my wife and who should I bump into, but that very referee. He spoke to me and quite candidly boasted that by selling stories about me to the papers, he had earned a good deal of money. 'Yes, I made a lot of money out of you,' he said with a smug grin on his face.

Fortunately, referees like that are the exception rather than the rule, but I do not hold with the innocent image that is sometimes given them. I do not believe that a man should be publicly abused just because he is a referee but, by the same token, there are some pretty poor referees in charge of important games and sometimes it is their protection that seems to be paramount in the eyes of the establishment. A team can be subjected to the most abysmal refereeing but if any player or manager dares to say as much he is almost immediately in hot water with the FA. Sometimes, it seems, there does not appear to be any real justice.

I had been under suspension for only a week when the news broke that I had been named 'European Footballer of the Year' for 1964. It was wonderful. In a way it is not only exciting but humbling too when something like that happens to you. I still keep that award in a safe place because of how much it means to me. When I received it those Aberdeen trawlers seemed so very far away, yet I could not help thinking that maybe they would be sharing in my delight and be a part of it.

As 1964 ended, Manchester United were poised to stake a claim for the championship. We had at last struck a vein of form. Since the early hiccups there had been only one defeat in 20 games. We had beaten Tottenham 4–1, Wolves 4–2 and Aston Villa 7–0. I remember that match in particular because I scored four goals. I also remember the defeat. It was at home to Leeds, one of our keenest rivals in the race for the championship. It may sound like sour grapes when I say that we probably lost due to the fog. The referee stopped the game and took us all off the pitch for ten minutes, at a time when we were virtually running the show. Only Gary Sprake in the Leeds goal was keeping us at bay. George Best hit the crossbar and, a little later, had to leave the pitch because of an injury. Not only did we lose the points to our rivals but it also helped them to consolidate their lead at the top of the table.

We had made progress in the Fairs Cup, as it was then known. In the first round we had knocked out Djurgaarden with a 7–2 aggregate. In the next round we went even further by beating Borussia Dortmund with a 10–2 aggregate scoreline, and that set us up for a third round tie with Everton.

So, as 1965 began, we were third in the table behind Leeds and Chelsea, and we also had interests in two major cup competitions. I kept on training while I was suspended and by the time I was able to return I felt like a greyhound in the trap, waiting for the hare to go past and get the race going.

My great day arrived on 16 January 1965 when I was back in a United shirt for the visit to Nottingham Forest. I scored after three minutes, thanks to a well-rehearsed move from a free-kick which involved Bobby Charlton and David Herd. The game ended at 2–2 and I also scored our other goal. It was a great feeling to be back on the pitch and scoring meant that much more to me.

Looking back, a break of 28 days does not seem that long but, at the time, I remember it felt like a very long time indeed. It makes me glad that there were no mid-season breaks in my day, except for those times of really severe weather.

With Scotland having tried a mid-season break, I'm sure that it will not be long before the whole of British football will be doing the same thing. I can see the advantages in that you won't suffer the frustrations of cancelled matches – but a pre-determined break can have a bad psychological effect on a team that is going well. It's not only that. If you are going to have a month off you will either have to extend your season, and therefore cut down on the summer break, or else you have to reduce the number of fixtures – and that doesn't seem to be an option that anyone, other than players, would welcome.

I was glad to have been match-fit for my return because the games were coming thick and fast. A few days after the draw at Forest we were at home to Everton for the first leg of our Fairs Cup third round tie. We drew 1–1 and then met Stoke at home in the League three days later for another 1–1 draw. A few days after that we played away to them in the FA Cup fourth round. Since that ended as a 0–0 draw we played them yet again four days later in a replay, which we won 1–0. Three days later we lost 0–1 in a League match at Tottenham. Then we travelled to Goodison Park for the Fairs Cup return leg, which we won 2–1, and followed that with a tough League match at home to Burnley. We won 3–2 and put our feet up for a week before our FA Cup fifth round match – also against Burnley.

From the moment that I had returned to the side we had played eight major games in 28 days. For me it could not have been any more extreme. I had endured 28 days without a game and followed that with 28 days of non-stop action. Having a whole week to prepare for our FA Cup meeting with Burnley was almost like having a holiday.

Burnley took the lead in the match and shut up shop. We had terrible trouble in breaking them down and, with less than ten minutes to go, we were beginning to wonder what we had to do to score. The answer was unorthodox, to say the least. Besty got the ball and we noticed that he was holding one of his boots which had come off just before he received the ball. George took control, grinned at us, and calmly stroked a perfect pass, with his bootless foot, to Pat Crerand. He floated over a beauty of a cross and I bicycle-kicked it into the net. A minute later Paddy smacked in a long-range shot and we won 2–1.

The pace was hotting up more and more as the season wore on. We hit a really good spell of League results which included a 3–0 win over Wolves, followed by a 4–0 win over our rivals, Chelsea, and then a 4–1 win over their West London neighbours, Fulham. A couple of weeks later we hit five against Blackburn. It was not just that we were scoring goals, we were also playing good, adventurous football. George Best's reputation and popularity were growing with every sparkling performance.

We did have our bad days as well of course and kicked ourselves for single-goal defeats by Sunderland and Sheffield Wednesday, which were the only flaws in a run of 11 victories in 13 League matches. There was never a major scene if we lost, unless we were heavily beaten. Matt always remained calm and would send us out for the next game telling us that we were great individual players as well as being a great team – so we were to get out there and show everyone what we could do. If there was ever any raging to be done, or hysteria to be whipped up, Jimmy Murphy was the man.

Jimmy added the salt to Busby's sugar. Don't get me wrong, Matt was a tough character and it took a lot to face him down. For all that, he was a gentleman and he liked to build up his own players rather than rubbish the opposition. Jimmy Murphy didn't care what he had to say. He would call the opposition, call the club cat, tell us that we'd better shape up – or else. He would lash out at anything and anybody. Yet he was not just huff and puff. He was a tremendous assistant manager who could put fire in your belly but still be there to offer a shoulder to cry on if it became necessary. The combination of Busby and Murphy was the best – and that is taking nothing at all away from Alex Ferguson, who has proved beyond any doubt that he, above all others, has earned the right to be mentioned in the same breath as Busby and Murphy.

While we were battling on the League front, we were also very busy in the FA Cup and the Fairs Cup. At the end of March we were due to face Leeds in the semi-final of the FA Cup at Hillsborough. They were our chief rivals for the championship too, so both teams were, in fact, within reach of the 'double'. With so much at stake I suppose it was almost inevitable that both sides would be tremendously wound up before the game.

Hillsborough was packed with 65,000 fans and the atmosphere was incredible. Within the first few minutes, the tension boiled over. I was going for a ball but my shirt was not going with me. Jack Charlton had grabbed a handful of it and was trying to hold me back. It was literally being ripped off my back. It seemed that I was to be the first victim of the Leeds tactics of taking out the major threats and then imposing pressure on the rest. I lashed out at Jack and we began swapping punches. I was unaware that our team-mates had immediately joined in the fray, and there were fists flying all over the place. It took a few minutes for the referee, Dick Windle, to calm the situation down, but I cannot help feeling that if he had blown his whistle the moment Jack Charlton claimed my shirt as a souvenir, there would have been a different complexion to the whole game.

107

As it was there were flare-ups throughout the 90 minutes, which meant that our normal free-flowing style of football was completely thwarted. No goals were scored and, at the end of the match, everyone trooped off in a bad mood. I never enjoyed playing against Leeds United. Few people did. But it has to be said that I did hold players like Jack Charlton and Billy Bremner in the highest esteem. It was their tactics and gamesmanship that I could not stand. They could play very good football and often did but they seemed to believe that they needed to intimidate people, or put them out of the game, before they could begin to play properly. They also used to pull all sorts of strokes to confuse referees. But what a team Don Revie had put together. They were certainly one of the greatest sides of all time.

We did not look forward to having to meet them again in the replay – but there was no avoiding it. We turned up at the City Ground, Nottingham, still annoyed at the treatment we had received at Hillsborough a few days earlier. Both sides adopted a much calmer approach and concentrated on kicking the ball rather than each other. It always sounds like sour grapes to say that you were the better side on the day even though you lost, but I defy anyone to say otherwise about that particular game. Gary Sprake was in terrific form in the Leeds goal and certainly did not have 'careless hands' that day. Leeds also had the woodwork on their side. I'm convinced that the posts and bar were heading the ball away.

We dominated but could not get the ball into the net. Then, as extra-time seemed inevitable, our former team-mate, Johnny Giles, sent a great free-kick into our area. Someone tried to clear, the ball struck the back of Billy Bremner's head and ricocheted into our net. We couldn't believe it. Bremner's goal had taken the FA Cup away from us.

The loss made us all the more determined to be successful in the League. Our Fairs Cup campaign was on hold for a while, so we were able to concentrate more fully on the run-in to the League Championship. Most people thought that Leeds would win it, but we were by no means out of it and Chelsea also were still a threat. Looking back, Leeds had the title in the palms of their hands. After they had knocked us out of the FA Cup, we had that 5–0 away win over Blackburn. Then we beat Leicester 1–0 before having to play Leeds again in the return First Division game at Elland Road. Despite our good form they were still three points clear of us at the top of the table. They had that psychological advantage, plus the knowledge that they had won at Old Trafford and had ended our FA Cup hopes. We were all the more determined that they would not have the last laugh.

There was a relaxed but very positive atmosphere in our dressing room. We knew what to expect from Leeds and we were more than ready for it. The game itself was another tough encounter and it had 0–0 written all over it until John Connelly pumped the ball home for the only goal of the game. We were ecstatic. We knew that there was still work to be done but we had just burst through one of our major obstacles. If you had been in our dressing room afterwards you would have thought that we had just won the championship itself. Leeds had been unbeaten for five months – but not any more.

A few days later we were on our travels again. This time we were at St Andrews to face Birmingham City. We had drawn with them at Old Trafford but we were well aware that every point counted and another draw would not really be good enough. It was Easter Monday, but there was no Bank Holiday for us. We meant business, and to prove it we won 4–2. That just about ended Birmingham's season, for a couple of weeks later they were relegated, having finished at the bottom of the table. It was an extremely sweet victory for us because both Leeds and Chelsea lost, and that meant that we were at the top of the First Division with just three games left to play.

Liverpool were next on our agenda. They had already reached the FA Cup Final and were out of the title race but were still keen to take maximum points from Old Trafford. We had other ideas of course. Late in the first half I scored our first goal and that relaxed us for the second half. Matt told us to stay calm and keep on playing the same way and we would score more in the second half. As usual he was right, as I found out to my cost.

As well as holding one arm aloft in salute, I had another habit when I scored. Whenever possible I liked to follow the ball into the net. We hadn't been playing very long in the second half when Pat Crerand sent over a great cross which I turned into the goal to make it 2–0. I ran into the net to follow it and collided with the stanchion, which gashed my knee. It hurt like hell, and I couldn't believe it when I looked down at the gaping wound. So that put paid to getting a hat-trick as I had to go and have a few stitches in the injury. John Connelly made it 3–0 near the end which ensured that made sure that we kept our lead at the top of the First Division.

After the game I went home and put my feet up for the weekend before limping back to the ground on Monday morning. We were due to play Arsenal later that day for our last home fixture of the season. I had my injury investigated and I was strapped up again. I didn't think I could stand the tension of watching the game, so I decided to go home and wait for the result. As I was limping across the car park, Matt called me to him and asked where I was going. When I told him he smiled, shook his head and said, 'You'll no want to be missing the team talk!'

It took a moment for the penny to drop and then I suddenly realized that he wanted me to play. I'd had a chunk of metal pierce my knee just two days earlier and he wanted me to play. I did suggest to him that he must be joking of course, but Matt shook his head slowly and told me to get to the team talk.

So that is how I came to be playing against Arsenal. My knee was heavily strapped and did not feel at all its usual self but, I thought, if Matt believed that I could make some sort of a contribution then who was I to disagree. As it happened, after six minutes I put through the pass that led to Besty scoring our first goal. In the second half I scored with about half an hour left – and then got another later in the game which made the final score 3–1.

There are no words to describe the atmosphere. Old Trafford was at its most electric. It was not just the fact that we were winning but news was coming through via the supporters' transistor radios of what was happening at the other grounds. Every now and then we would hear a roar from the crowd and try to find out what it was about. That is how we heard that Leeds were losing 0–3 at Birmingham. Then they fought back to make it 3–3. You can imagine how the Old Trafford fans were reacting when they kept on hearing goal flashes on the radio.

That evening, Leeds were playing their last game of the season. They had to win to stand any chance of taking the title. We still had one game left, away to Aston Villa, but, if the score remained as it was, we would have to lose by a big margin for Leeds to take the title. The minutes ticked away – we were leading 3–1 and Leeds were still drawing 3–3. The tension was incredible and I hardly noticed how much my knee was throbbing. At long last the referee blew his whistle and, at exactly the same time, the referee at St Andrews ended the game there. Bar any stupid mistakes, we were champions of the League.

We were perhaps a little premature in our celebrations, but we couldn't help it. There was singing and dancing on the terraces and we joined in on the pitch. Matt was thrilled to pieces. It had been eight years since he had last celebrated winning the championship and a lot had happened since then, much of it still very painful in his memory. Who could deny him a smile of satisfaction?

I didn't play in the last game of the season at Aston Villa. We lost 1–2 but it didn't really matter. We were confirmed as champions because we had a better goal average than Leeds United, who finished as runners-up in both the League and the FA Cup.

We still had some Fairs Cup business to settle. We eventually got round to completing our quarter-final tie against Racing

Club of Strasbourg. We beat them 5–0 at their place and I scored twice. Before the return leg at Old Trafford I was presented with the 'European Footballer of the Year' award and, at the same time, we were formally handed the League Championship trophy. It was quite a night and I think the occasion got to us because the game ended in a 0–0 draw. It was a little disappointing that we did not manage to score one or two goals.

Almost immediately we were into semi-final action against Ferencvaros of Hungary, the first leg taking place at Old Trafford. They were a different proposition from the sides we had already met and beaten. They were skilful, but they were also very physical. It was a tough game but, with two goals from David Herd and one from yours truly, we beat them 3–2. We hoped that would give us the edge for the return leg.

The political system in Eastern Europe was different then and, because of rigid security, we were not allowed to land in Hungary. Instead we had to fly to Vienna and then go by coach to Budapest. When we came to the border we were held up for a couple of hours while everyone's papers were thoroughly examined and it all began to seem a little surreal because we appeared to be entering a world which consisted mostly of barbed wire and machine-guns. It was not a pleasant experience.

We played well in the return leg, despite a rainstorm, but still conceded the one goal that Ferencvaros needed to draw level. The away goals rule was not yet in operation in those days and so there had to be a replay. The two managers tossed a coin to find out who would have home advantage. Unfortunately Matt got it wrong. The replay was as tight as our other two encounters but in the end it was the Hungarians who won the day with a 2–1 result. At least the weather started to improve, and we were more than glad to be travelling home.

Ferencvaros went on to win the competition, beating Juventus in the final, and I was pleased about that because they deserved their success, and the Hungarian people also deserved something to bring them a smile or two. Having experienced, if only for a few days, what life was like for them, I have some idea of how joyful they must have felt when the old regime disintegrated and the barbed wire came down.

That ended our season. I had scored 28 goals in 36 League matches, three in six FA Cup games, and eight in ten European appearances. Most important, however, was the fact that it had been a great season for Manchester United. We were already looking forward to the next season when we would, once again, be competing in the big one – the European Cup. But for now we were thrilled to bits to know that we were the Champions of the Football League. Nice one!

9

ON THE LIST

Winning the championship might be considered to be the ultimate prize and, in many ways, I suppose it is because it is the reward for consistent hard work and good results over a period of many months. The trouble is, you can become addicted to winning the championship. When you have done it once you want to do it again, and again. There is no doubt in my mind that you can become very possessive over the championship and you definitely do not like the idea of anyone else having it for a season or two. Believe me, any notion that winning the title will satisfy your hunger, and make you less bothered the following season, is complete nonsense.

When we began the 1965–66 season we knew exactly what our assignment was. We had to win everything that we entered, which meant that we were gunning for the FA Cup, the European Cup, and the League Championship again. It was a tall order, but we were not going to neglect one competition in favour of another. If we had a priority at all it was the European Cup. I think we all wanted to win that for the club as well as for ourselves. There was an extra edge: we also wanted to win it for Matt after everything he had been through since his last attempt at the trophy. However, that did not mean that we would not be firing on all cylinders for the other competitions. If you don't make it in the European Cup, the best way to capitalize on your experience is to be competing again the following season, and the only way to do that – in those days – was to win the League.

Our summer preparations were quite normal, except that a pre-season friendly in Nuremberg had left me with a hip injury which was proving very slow in responding to treatment. I was extremely annoyed and frustrated at having to miss the opening couple of games of the season. After a 2–2 draw with Liverpool in the Charity Shield at Old Trafford, the scene was set for the new campaign to begin where the old one had finished. David Herd scored the first goal of the season as United beat Sheffield at home, but there was a shock in store for the trip to Nottingham Forest three days later. Pat Dunne in goal had a bit of a nightmare and Forest were leading 4–0 and threatening to score even more before United rallied to find the net twice. It was not good enough to avoid defeat but it served to stop what would have been a total disaster.

David Gaskell was put in goal for the next game at Northampton, and I'm pleased to say that I was finally able to make my first appearance of the season. For those who were not around at the time and might be wondering what Northampton were doing in the top division, they had just been promoted. They had reached the First Division in a meteoric rise, having left the Fourth in 1961 and gone through the next two divisions in just four seasons. We had no intention of taking them lightly but, it must be said, we probably did. John Connelly put us ahead and we sat back after that. Five minutes from the end they equalized. As we travelled back, we began to get the feeling that things were not going according to plan. By now we should have had far more than the three points we had earned from our opening three games.

I really started to worry after our next two matches. They were both at home and they both ended in draws. We had now played our first five games and I had not yet scored. I have never been a real worrier but you cannot help but get somewhat concerned when things are not going to plan. It changed a little when we travelled to Newcastle for our next fixture. The newspapers were full of United's announcement that profits were up, gate receipts were up and the club was in a very healthy position. Fleetingly it crossed my mind that my contract was up for renewal at the end of the season, and that perhaps there might be a better deal on the table if our success story were to continue. It was only a fleeting thought and I would not like anyone to get the impression that I was only interested in money. Playing for United came first, money could sort itself out later. We had a whole season to get through yet.

There has always been a bit of a stigma attached to being a professional footballer or an entertainer. I think it is worse these days than it was in the past, but we used to come in for some stick even when I was playing. The stigma involves money of course. Some people seem to have a problem getting it into their heads that we are professionals, paid for our skills in our particular way of life – just the same as surgeons, top executives and others. Because we do something that we would probably enjoy doing for nothing, there has always been an element that believes we play professionally only because money is the motivating force.

I learned from an early age that if a player wanted to make the most of his career he also had to take care of himself financially. I had not been a professional for very long when a major Sunday newspaper approached me to tell my life story. Looking back, it was absolutely ridiculous that they should want to serialize what had been only 17 years, yet they were perfectly serious. I asked a high fee. I was not being greedy and I did not mind talking to the press about the games but, if a newspaper was going to try to increase its circulation and attract more revenue on the strength of telling my story, I did not see why I should not have a share of their profits.

It was not a particularly high fee by today's standards and would not even be considered 'pocket-money', but the newspaper was quite shocked. There again, the editor had probably never lived in an Aberdeen tenement block, with eight other members of a family, surviving on less than ten pounds a week. I stuck to my guns and that probably created the image that I have sometimes been rather forceful when dealing with financial matters. I am not, and never have been, motivated by money, but I had too hard an upbringing to be a fool.

That was not on my mind when we travelled to Newcastle, though. All I wanted was to score a goal and get us back on track to fulfil our ambitions. From that point of view it was a completely successful trip. We won 2–1, with David Herd scoring one of our goals and me the other. It may not have been the most convincing of victories but I felt that I was back in business at last.

The mood was good in the dressing room after that win, but we were a bit shell-shocked after our next game when Burnley beat us 3–0 at Turf Moor. To say the least it was a poor performance from us and we were all ashamed of ourselves as we travelled home. There could be no excuses. After that we were at home to Newcastle, who were after revenge following our victory at St James's Park. They nearly got it too. Nobby Stiles scored our goal, but we had to be satisfied with a draw as Newcastle also found the net.

Our next home game was against Chelsea and there was a bit of a shock in store as Matt dropped George Best in favour of John Aston. I think the boss was trying to tell us something. At last we clicked and Chelsea got the full force of our efforts. I scored a hat-trick and we ran out 4–1 winners, which was a great relief to everyone.

A few days later we were on the European Cup trail with a trip to Finland, where we played HJK Helsinki. They were not expected to be a big problem but, in truth, they gave us a bit of a scare. We won 3–2 in the first leg, with John Connelly, David Herd and myself getting our goals. But they had some exceptional youngsters who played their hearts out and, if I tell you that I actually kicked off the line to stop them from equalizing, it will give you some idea of just how difficult a game we had. We made no mistake in the return leg at Old Trafford, though, and won 6–0, with John Connelly getting a hat-trick, to make it through to the next round with a 9–2 aggregate.

Our League form continued to be unpredictable. We lost 2–4 to Arsenal and beat Liverpool 2–0, so anyone looking at us as a safe bet for any kind of result would have been throwing away their money.

It was after the Liverpool game that I made a big mistake. My next match was for Scotland against Poland in a World Cup qualifier on 13 October 1965, at Hampden. We were going well in our group and were even more enthusiastic than usual, if that is possible, because we wanted to be part of the 1966 tournament which was being staged in England. Poland were already out of the competition because of their failures in the group matches but, since they had to play both ourselves and Italy, they could still have some say in the final outcome of the group.

It was a hard game and a very disappointing one too because we lost 1–2, despite having nearly all of the serious play. Poland scored two goals in the last five minutes, otherwise we would have gained the result we were seeking. And to make matters worse, I badly damaged my knee and came away from Hampden with it so swollen that I could hardly get my trousers on.

Manchester United had a rule then that players injured in an international had to report to Old Trafford as soon as possible afterwards for treatment. Well, Denis Law being Denis Law, I thought I knew better and I broke that rule. I thought that if I just rested the swelling would go down and that would be the end of it. I said nothing to anybody about the injury. I turned up at Old Trafford on Friday, two days after the game, just in time to join everyone else boarding the coach to London for our League match against Tottenham the following day.

My knee was still very painful when I woke up in our

London hotel, but I thought it would right itself and disguised it so that I could play. I was extremely foolish because, as the match wore on, it just became worse and worse. We took a 5–1 hammering from Tottenham that day but I was only involved in half the game because I could not carry on after half-time. John Fitzpatrick, also from Aberdeen, took my place and in doing so he created a little bit of history by becoming the first substitute ever used by Manchester United. I, of course, was the first player to be substituted. What a record!

The knee gave me trouble for years after that. I don't know if it would have been any different had I stuck to the club rules and gone for immediate attention, but I certainly made a mistake in not doing the right thing and at least letting someone try to get it sorted out before it became worse. I finally had an operation more than two years later in 1968, but really the knee was never the same again.

I missed the next couple of games and returned for a League match at home to Blackburn. Harry Gregg was back in the side by now. He had missed all the previous season because of a shoulder injury, but he had reclaimed his place and, but for a couple of games, he was to remain our goalkeeper for the rest of the season. No disrespect, either to Pat Dunne or David Gaskell, but I think Harry gave the defence that little bit more confidence. Either that or he shouted at them a lot more – whatever, it worked.

We put together a decent run of results which included a 5–1 revenge over Tottenham just before Christmas, and victories over Everton and Sunderland. We were back among the goals too, as six against Northampton and five against Leicester proved. From the middle of October to the end of March we suffered just two defeats in 20 League matches. We also began our FA Cup campaign and disposed of Derby County in the third round with a 5–2 victory at their place. We went on to beat Rotherham, Wolverhampton Wanderers and Preston to reach the semi-final, where we were to meet Everton.

Meanwhile, in the European Cup, we knocked out ASK

Vorwaerts, of what was then East Germany, by winning both legs of the tie. Our prize for that was to be drawn against the mighty Benfica in the next round. Nobody wanted to face Benfica; they were the one team that we all wanted to avoid. However, having been drawn out of the hat with them, there was not a lot we could do about it.

The first leg took place at Old Trafford and Benfica were every bit as strong as we had been led to believe. We rose to the occasion, though, and won 3–2 on the night. But for a late goal from Torres we would have had a two-goal advantage for the return leg in Lisbon. Nobody was prepared to give us any hope when that lead was reduced to a single goal.

The trip to the magnificent Stadium of Light was a little daunting because the Benfica fans thronged around us as we drove slowly through. I had experienced something like this in Italy but for some of my team-mates it was somewhat unnerving. The Benfica supporters kept holding up five fingers at us. It was not a rude gesture but a reminder that on our last trip to Lisbon, their neighbours – Sporting Lisbon – had put five goals past us. At least, we hoped that was what they meant.

We were all keyed up and rarin' to go as kick-off time approached but we were kept waiting for a further 20 minutes while Eusébio was presented with his trophy as 'European Footballer of the Year' for 1965. I could not grumble. I had won it the previous year and someone else had been forced to wait. Besides, I don't think that anyone could have failed to applaud the award being presented to him. He was a tremendous player and a thoroughly nice guy.

That wasn't going through our minds at the time of course. We were just eager to get on with it. When the referee finally did blow his whistle to get the game under way, he unleashed a Manchester United side that was just amazing. That might sound a bit conceited since I was a part of that side but, if you have any doubts at all, get hold of a video of the game.

Within a quarter of an hour Benfica were reeling like a champion boxer who has been floored by a surprise attack. Besty scored twice and John Connelly hit another and in that short space of time we were 3–0 ahead. Benfica did not know what had hit them. Bobby Charlton and Pat Crerand added a goal apiece in the second half to make the final score 5–1 – but it was George's night. He totally destroyed the Benfica defence with a display that made even the players of both sides applaud. They just could not stop him, by either fair means or foul. He left everyone for dead time after time. It was probably one of the finest individual performances by a professional footballer – or indeed by any sportsman – that I have ever witnessed. George was fantastic!

The following day the newspapers ran out of superlatives. Photographs of George with that famous film-star grin of his were flashed around the world, with the title of El Beatle used by virtually all the press. Everyone knew about the Beatles, but now there was a new one – a footballing Beatle. George's life would never be the same again. He had proved himself a world-class player, but now he was a world-wide superstar as well.

The Times reporter wrote: 'This was the most inspired, inspiring and controlled performance I have ever seen by any British side abroad in the last 20 years. Had I not seen it I would not have believed it.'

That was typical of the press response, except for one of the Portuguese newspapers which went against the tide a little and said simply that we should have won because the game was invented in Britain and our performance was no more than it should have been. Well, you can't please them all, can you?

Our feet were firmly put back on the ground when we went to Chelsea for our next game. They beat us 2–0 and again our championship hopes suffered another dent. We bounced back with a victory over Arsenal but we then began a run of high-pressure games which were to ruin our season.

Having drawn against Aston Villa we were beaten at home by Leicester City, past whom we had put five goals some

121

months earlier. I was still having trouble with my knee and missed the Leicester game – and George too was having similar trouble. His knee had been injured in the FA Cup quarter-final against Preston, when he was brought down heavily from behind. He had been receiving intensive treatment but the footballing world was nowhere near as knowledgeable about injuries then as it is today. George's knee had not responded to treatment and, after hobbling around in the game against Leicester, his season was effectively over.

And so we travelled to Partizan Belgrade for the first leg of our European Cup semi-final. Before the game we had been favourites to win the European Cup after that victory in Lisbon, but Partizan took full advantage of our weaknesses as we would have done of theirs and we lost 0–2. With a two-goal deficit to make up, we were looking far from favourites at the end of the 90 minutes.

A League defeat against Sheffield United followed the defeat in Belgrade. A few days later Partizan travelled to Old Trafford well aware that they had only to protect their lead to get through to the final. We tried everything to break them down but they just packed their defence and held on. Nobby Stiles scored a few minutes from the end and there was a frantic last assault – but the scoreline remained at 1–0 and we were out. It was a big disappointment.

We had to lift ourselves straight away because, three days later, we had another important game. We travelled to Burnden Park to meet Everton in the FA Cup semi-final. Everton were in trouble for having fielded what was virtually a reserve side in their previous League match, but they shrugged that off and were happy to be able to put out a full-strength, fresh team to play against us. We were still reeling from the heavy programme of fixtures and travelling that we had faced in recent weeks and the result was that we lost a scrappy game by the only goal of the match, scored by Colin Harvey. Another trophy disappeared from view.

Just to finish off a lousy month for us, we lost 2–3 at West Ham and there was now no chance that we were going to retain the championship. We finished the season with a good run of results which included a 4–1 win at Blackburn and a 6–1 victory at home to Aston Villa. I missed both because of injury but I returned for our last fixture of the season, a home 1–1 draw with Leeds, which guaranteed us fourth place. At the end of that game we waved to our supporters and thanked them for all the help they had given us throughout our various campaigns. As always they had been magnificent and we were sorry that we had not brought them back at least one trophy to admire and rejoice over.

For me personally it was a miserable end to the season. I had a dodgy knee which had reduced my goal tally to 15 in 33 League matches. I had seen the three major trophies of our campaign slip away one by one, and I had seen Scotland fail to qualify for the World Cup finals. Still, at least nothing else could go wrong, could it?

Yes, it could. I had made another mistake. It was probably one of the biggest mistakes of my life. Having become accustomed to huge crowds at Old Trafford and seeing United go so far in the various competitions, I thought that my new contract should be substantially better and that I should receive a signing-on fee for putting my signature to it. I said as much to Matt in a letter and added that if I did not get what I wanted I would leave the club. I have often asked myself since why I adopted that tone. I was very happy at Old Trafford and the last thing that I wanted was to leave. I must have worked myself into a bad mood to write that letter because it was not my heart talking at all.

I heard nothing for a while and went back to Aberdeen for the summer break. Di was expecting our second child but, even so, I managed to get in a bit of golf. You can imagine what it was like when the golf course was suddenly besieged by a horde of photographers and reporters. They already knew something which I didn't – I had been transfer-listed.

It came as a bit of a shock, I can tell you. I had not expected the boss to take me at my word, and I certainly had not expected him to make a public announcement before we had had the chance to discuss it further. In my opinion he had made an error of judgement but he was probably trying to teach me a lesson – and not just me but anyone else who might start to think that they were bigger than Manchester United. I honestly did not think that but, on reflection, I can see how it might have looked that way.

The day after the press story broke I received his letter in response to mine. I wished that he had waited the 24 hours that it took for it to reach me, but there was no point in crying over spilt milk. I went into hiding for a day or two and then flew to Manchester for a face-to-face meeting with Matt Busby. It was an amicable meeting and we thrashed out a new deal. I know that there has been talk of my eating humble pie and so on, but it was not like that at all. Matt Busby was not the sort of person who expected that from his players. He treated you with respect and like a gentleman. I knew that I might have really got myself into trouble if Matt had turned nasty and insisted that I leave. That was the last thing I would have wanted. Fortunately for me he did not want me to leave either. We sat down and had a very pleasant chat and were able to come to a compromise which resulted in my getting a pay rise but no signing-on fee. The press were informed that the matter had been resolved and that Denis Law would not be leaving Old Trafford. Nobody was happier than me.

I have always been an individual who sorted out his own business. I believed that if you were not happy with your contract then it was your own fault, but that once you had agreed to do something you should see it through to its conclusion. In my case, at that time, my contract was coming to an end and I simply wanted to move with the times and better myself financially while I still had the chance.

I flew back to Aberdeen to welcome my second child into

the world, content in the knowledge that a disaster had been averted and that I was going to continue to be a Manchester United player for some time to come. Who could ask for more?

10

CHAMPIONS AGAIN

The summer of 1966 was spoiled for me by one momentous event – England won the World Cup. I was enjoying my summer break, having become a dad for the second time and sorted out the problem with United, so I did not let the news ruin everything, but it was nevertheless hard to swallow.

I am not one of those Scots who are fanatically anti-England. I do not subscribe to that attitude at all, but I still looked upon England as the Auld Enemy and I always enjoyed playing against them – especially when we beat them. I did not want them to win the World Cup because I knew that we would never hear the end of it. I was right too. But let us put the whole thing into perspective.

Winning the World Cup is supposed to be a tremendous achievement, proving to the rest of the world that you are the best there is – the champions of all football. To do that, you really have to win it on someone else's territory. Take the 1998 World Cup. France had everything going for them. They did not have to qualify, they had a fairly easy group and, even after they had squeezed into the final, it took a strangely off-colour performance by Brazil to hand France the World Cup on a plate.

It was just the same in 1966. England automatically qualified by being the host nation. Their group was not particularly strong since they had to get the best of Uruguay, Mexico and

France. Only Uruguay had any pedigree in those days and that was not great. In the opening game England were held to a 0–0 draw and did not look very good. A late goal by Uruguay would have been disaster for England, but that didn't happen. In the next game they were having all kinds of trouble trying to break down Mexico until Bobby Charlton scored with a great opportunist goal from some distance. Until that moment it was touch and go and, for my money, it could easily have ended with another 0–0 draw. The final group game was against France and they were a very weak side. It was little wonder that England won 2–0 and finished top of the group by one point from Uruguay.

Had the group finished with England in second place they would have had to go to Hillsborough to play against West Germany in the quarter-final. The entire history of the World Cup would have been completely different because there would never have been that exciting final between the two countries at Wembley. As it was, England met Argentina at Wembley in the amazing quarter-final during which the Argentinian captain, Antonio Ratin, was sent off. England scored the only goal of the game but deserved that victory for continuing to play football despite the provocation.

Portugal were next in line and my team-mate, Bobby Charlton, scored England's two goals as they won their way through to the final. Portugal scored one and were great entertainment value, but England had the edge throughout, especially in defence where they gave very little away.

So to the final, and extra time with the score at 2–2 after 90 minutes. There is still some controversy over whether or not the ball crossed the line for England's third goal and all the computer re-enactments in the world will not prove the point one way or another. A great Geoff Hurst goal sealed the matter anyway, and in the end British football was given a real boost by England winning the World Cup. I just wish they had done it overseas.

If you are English and reading this you probably think that

it is all sour grapes and that I am being unfair. Just step back from being English for a while and try to take an impartial view of the matter. If you do, you will see that England's work in winning the 1966 World Cup certainly did contain some individual moments of sheer brilliance, but it is always debatable whether any team winning the World Cup on home ground can truly earn the right to be called the best in the world.

That is why I could not be bothered with watching the World Cup Final. I knew England would win – they had to. That is why I went and played golf instead. It was a great afternoon because everyone else was glued to the television and my pal, John Hogan, and myself had the course at Chorlton-cum-Hardy all to ourselves. We had had a long-standing bet on who would win a game of golf between us. A condition of that bet was that I would be able to choose where and when. I chose the afternoon of the World Cup Final quite deliberately – but what a rotten afternoon it turned out to be! I lost my bet and, when I arrived back in the clubhouse, the whole place was going crazy. I guessed that it was not some sort of celebration because of the news that I'd lost my bet and, when they did tell me what it was they were celebrating, I threw my clubs down on the ground and simply said, 'Bastards!'

England had won the World Cup with a system that relied heavily on a defensive 4-3-3 style, which had all the excitement of a waterlogged cricket pitch. As a result, others followed the example and football took a distinct turn for the worse. With wingers gone there were no more surging runs and forward-line cavalry charges. Everything became robotic. Thank goodness that Alex Ferguson likes wingers and has allowed the talents of players like Ryan Giggs to give us back some of the thrills and spills of football.

England have never managed to win the World Cup since their 1966 triumph and there has been no joy in the European Champion either even when, in 1996, the odds were heavily stacked in England's favour. Penalties seem to be bad news for

England. The only realistic glimmer England have had was in the 1990 World Cup, when I thought that Bobby Robson was desperately unlucky not to go all the way with his men.

What about Scotland, you might say. Well, we have never had the advantages that England had in winning the 1966 World Cup. We have always had to do everything the hard way, so I don't think that anyone can point a finger and say that Scotland should have done better. There have been times when Scotland *could* have done better – but *should* have is a different matter.

Given all this, you may be able to see why we were all so delighted to beat England at Wembley in 1967. It put them in their place and it was a bit of fun to be able to tease them by saying that we were now the world champions because we were the first team to beat them after their World Cup victory.

Before that great day we had a new season with Manchester United to tackle, and the special challenge of attempting to regain the League Championship. We had our customary pre-season tour and it threw up a major problem. Harry Gregg had proven himself to be the pick of our goalkeepers but he was going through torture with every game because of the shoulder injury which had been plaguing him for the last couple of years. On that tour he let in 13 goals and it was certainly an unlucky number for him because Matt set about signing a new goalie. He came up with Alex Stepney.

The tour had not been a success. We played Celtic and lost 1–4. We played Bayern Munich and lost by the same score. Then we played FK Austria Vienna and lost 2–5. Nobby Stiles was sent off in that game but he probably enjoyed the rest because, only a few weeks earlier, Bobby Charlton, John Connelly and himself had been in England's World Cup squad.

Those three were given a special welcome when we opened the season against West Bromwich Albion at Old Trafford. The rest of us formed a guard of honour and applauded them on to the field. I respected and admired them as individuals, but I didn't hurt my hands too much as I applauded. Ironically, the season was not very old when Matt sold John Connelly to Blackburn Rovers. He did not seem to think that he had quite the strength for Manchester United. I liked having John in the side because he was a dab hand at long-range shots which goal-keepers spilled and yours truly had only to stab into the net.

Dave Gaskell was given the job of goalkeeper to start the season as Harry Gregg was having more treatment for his dodgy shoulder. Pat Crerand was also out for the first few games and John Fitzpatrick took his place. I felt much better and Besty was back as well, so we had a strong side for the opening game. We gave West Brom quite a lot to think about because the match was only a minute old when George took hold of the ball from Bobby Charlton and put us into the lead. A bit of an avalanche followed and the score went to 5-1 in the first 20 minutes.

It was an amazingly hot day and we eased off in the second half, which allowed West Brom to pull back two more goals. The scoring ended at 5-3 and we had got off to a winning start. It was especially nice because there had been a presentation to Jimmy Murphy before the game to commemorate his 20 years at Old Trafford and it was good to crown his day with a deci-sive victory.

Our next match was at Everton and it was a very different kind of game. It was not long before the pitch began to look more like a Roman arena with gladiators pairing off to fight each other. There were personal duels breaking out all over the place. Finally the referee called the two captains, Brian Labone and myself, together to order us to calm things down or he would have to take decisive action.

You cannot go round to each of your team-mates and relay to them what has just been said, but it did have the desired effect. When the other players saw the referee talking to the two captains they knew what was happening and changed their course accordingly. It wouldn't have mattered if the referee was simply asking the two captains who had won the 2.30 race at Sandown – it was the gesture that counted.

Everton were in the lead until 20 minutes from the end when I headed home a cross from David Herd. With the match poised at 1–1, Charlton tried a last-ditch strike. The ball rebounded and there was I to put it in the net. I think that's why they sometimes called me 'The Demon King' – I kept popping up when nobody was expecting me. That second goal against Everton was a special one for me because it was my 100th League goal for the club in 139 games.

We suffered a defeat at Leeds which once again threw up questions about our defence. However, when Everton paid us a return visit we won 3–0 and all seemed right with the world again. Harry Gregg returned for what would be his last two games for Manchester United. We won the first 3–2 against Newcastle but then lost at Stoke. Harry never played for United again and began a successful career in coaching and management. It was also John Connelly's last game. The following match ended in another League defeat at Tottenham and it was the turn of Dave Gaskell to play his last game in goal for United.

We were back in the League Cup that season. It was only the second time that Manchester United had entered, the first having been in the inaugural season of the competition. We were due to play away to Blackpool, who were a First Division club in those days. I was not playing but I went along to see the match and sat next to Alex Stepney, who had just joined us and was awaiting his début.

I did not know him but we were now team-mates and I tried to be sociable. The problem was that Alex was trying to show enthusiasm and learn as much as possible. He kept talking and asking questions. He could not have picked a worse person to sit alongside. I am better now but, when I was playing, I could never really stand to watch a game – especially if my team was getting beaten. Alex must have thought that I was going to be a pretty poor kind of team-mate when all he got in answer to his questions and remarks was a series of disinterested grunts. The truth is I was just too keyed up. I was always like it and when half-time came I went down to get a cup of tea and never returned to my seat. I hovered around the back of the stands, turning from tea to cigarette and back again until it was all over. We lost 1–5 and there was no excuse for that kind of scoreline, even though we did have several reserves playing. Pat Dunne was in goal and that was his last game for the United first team.

When Alex Stepney stepped out at Old Trafford a few days later for his début, he was already the fourth goalkeeper to play in the United first team that season, and his three colleagues had all played their last senior games for the club by then. The season was less than a month old.

I never did ask him, but I wonder if Alex was aware of all that when he walked out to make his début in – of all games – the local derby against City. We had not played a League match against them since my first season at Old Trafford because City had been relegated. They were back now, though, and the old rivalry had resumed.

There is always a lot of tension in derby games. This one was no exception. City were not a good side and probably on any other day against a similar team we would have had a much more convincing scoreline. As it was, we won 1–0 with yours truly scoring the decisive goal. For Alex Stepney it was a great début. He was soon in action and showed confident hands when the City forwards tested him. For a goalkeeper to come off the pitch at the end of his début having kept a clean sheet, especially in a local derby like that one, was definitely a cause for celebration.

Our next game was also at home, against Burnley. We had said farewell to John Connelly the day before as he packed his bags and followed his career to Blackburn. With John gone, John Aston came into the side on a more regular basis as a left-sided winger. This meant that George Best was able to take up his favoured position on the right wing. I scored our opening goal against Burnley with an overhead kick and we went on to win 4–1. My goal meant that I had now scored nine in as many

First Division games. My knee felt good and my confidence was brimming.

I missed our next game, which was a 1–4 defeat at Nottingham Forest where Johnny Carey was the manager. Carey had played for United many years earlier and if ever a man wanted to be manager of the club, that man was Johnny Carey. It was unfortunate that he was born at the wrong time because I think he would probably have been very good for Manchester United – had we not already got the best.

By now we were into early October and Chelsea were top of the First Division with an unbeaten run. Spurs were second and Stoke City were breathing down their necks. United were around seventh in the table and we knew that we had to become more consistent if we were going to make an impact on the championship race. I returned for our game against Blackpool and scored both our goals as we won 2–1. We then drew 1–1 at home with our title rivals Chelsea and again I scored our goal. When we beat Arsenal in our next outing we began a run of six straight victories and that gave our championship claim a real boost.

I did not play in all those games. In fact I missed the visit to Chelsea, which we won 3–1. That was very annoying. Not the victory of course, but the reason why I was unable to play. I had stubbed my toe in training the day before. It was ridiculous and I probably sound like some sort of wimp but it really hurt and anyone who earns a living from kicking things will tell you that your kicking is not quite its usual self if you have to keep hopping around with your damaged toe held in the air.

I missed only that one game during the run but I found myself acting as a foil for the others in some of the matches. I did not mind that. Football is a team game and, while all the best scorers are greedy for goals, they must also work for their team-mates and be prepared to step aside whenever or wherever it becomes necessary. I stepped aside four times for David Herd when we played at home to Sunderland. We beat them 5–0 and I scored a beauty of a goal while David scored four fluky ones – er, I'm only joking, David.

Sheffield United ruined our Christmas that year. Apart from a 1–2 defeat at Aston Villa we had been undefeated since the beginning of October. We went to Bramall Lane on Boxing Day and they beat us 2–1, which was a bit unsporting, so we had to take it out on them the following day in the return match at Old Trafford. We won 2–0 and that re-established our form as we were never beaten again that season in the League.

Bobby Noble came into the United side in defence that season and made a brilliant start to his career. I had played against him in training and was convinced he was destined to become one of the all-time greats. He was a product of the United youth set-up and they had uncovered an absolute gem. He made his début, I think against Blackpool, and he played as if he had been in the First Division for years. Tragically, in April 1967, he was involved in a car crash and it ended his career. I think football lost a great deal that day.

There was also a sickening injury to David Herd during that season. He was firing on all cylinders and would probably have ended up as our top scorer until he was involved in a collision with Gordon Banks and Graham Cross of Leicester. You could hear the crack echo around Old Trafford. When I saw it I thought his career was over. He did eventually come back the following season but he was never quite the same again and was later transferred to Stoke. Again it was a great loss because David was such a tremendous goal-scorer. It underlines what I was saying earlier about football careers: you never know when they are going to end or whether they will be seriously affected by an accident.

Talking about injuries – as the season wore on I was experiencing more trouble with my knee. I sometimes had pain-killing injections and sometimes had ice put on the knee to deaden it for the game. I can even remember standing for three-quarters of an hour while cold water was run over it from a tap so that it became numbed before I tried to run on it. The things you do to earn a living.

It was my knee which caused me to miss some matches. One

which I would like to have been excluded from was our FA Cup fourth round tie at home to Norwich City. We had beaten Stoke in the third round and it did not seem that Norwich, a Second Division side, would present us with much of a problem in front of our own supporters. They did, though. The Canaries defended as if their lives depended upon it and we managed only one goal. They caught us on the hop twice and knocked us out of the competition with a 2–1 result which really hurt. We took some flak from various quarters after that but it made us all the more determined to win the League.

I continued to score fairly regularly, but there were several of us finding the net now. Our position in the First Division table continued to be good but Liverpool were proving to be a bit of a thorn in our side. Every time we took the top spot they would get another win and knock us off again. Nottingham Forest, Tottenham and Leeds were also still in the hunt, so the title race was wide open as we entered the last quarter of the season. We drew 0–0 at Liverpool, so that did not prove anything one way or the other because our earlier meeting at Old Trafford had also ended in a draw. The week before had seen our 5–2 win at home to Leicester and Bobby Charlton had received the 'European Footballer of the Year' award and a special award for being the best player in the 1966 World Cup. It gives you a lift when you see a team-mate being honoured like that. I just wished that Bobby had been born in Scotland.

We took three points from four in our Bank Holiday double-header with Fulham and then had to play West Ham at home. By now Liverpool had faded a little and our nearest rivals were Nottingham Forest, who remained two points behind us. We were clear leaders of the division but we could not open a real gap between ourselves and the rest of the pack. The record books show that we beat West Ham 3–0 and I scored one of the goals – but that does not tell the whole story.

We were totally dominant throughout the game but it was not until the last couple of minutes that we went from 1–0 to 3–0. We had done everything except run up a huge list of goals throughout the rest of the game. To give you some idea, we were awarded a penalty and yours truly took it. I did everything right but I still managed to miss. Believe me, missing a penalty in front of thousands of people is one of the worst feelings imaginable. You feel really dreadful. I wanted a hole to appear and swallow me up but there is no hiding place while you imagine everyone is pointing at you and using just one word. I'll leave you to decide upon the word.

I don't know if it was the tension, but we went off the boil a little after that win against West Ham. We drew at Sheffield Wednesday, but it was not convincing and we were grateful that our rivals were going through the same sort of problem. A 3–0 win over Southampton gave us another confidence boost and we then drew 0–0 at Sunderland.

The visit of Aston Villa was a bit of fun, if you like that sort of thing. We won 3–1 but that was not the whole story by any means. During the match the Villa defenders seemed to be taking it in turns to kick me. I felt as if I was the subject of a club sweepstake to see who could put the most bruises on my legs. I never did learn to keep quiet and just get on with the game and I found that I was having a series of off-the-ball punch-ups throughout the match. The referee seemed to be in serious need of a visit to Specsavers because he appeared to see nothing. Then, in the second half, I had a goal disallowed for an alleged off-side. There were at least three players between me and the goal, so if that was off-side then I'm an ex-England international. I said something along those lines to the referee and he put me in the book. All that kicking and slapping that had been going on and he showed me a yellow card for raising a valid point about an off-side decision. I was a bit grumpy as well because my feet hurt. I was using different boots and they were not as comfortable as my old ones, especially with size nine Villa boots trampling all over them every now and then. Five minutes from the end I took my boots off and carried them for the rest of the game.

We had just two matches left and we were still top of the

table, but we had not yet placed ourselves beyond the reach of Nottingham Forest. We needed at least a point from our last but one game away to West Ham. It was to prove a memorable occasion because we were fired up for it. On the day 38,424 fans turned up – the biggest crowd at Upton Park since before the Second World War.

Once the whistle blew we went to work with a vengeance. Within two minutes Bobby Charlton had put us ahead. Pat Crerand made it 2–0 after five and then Bill Foulkes scored to make it 3–0 with only ten minutes gone. The visiting supporters were going crazy. It was not just that we scored the goals, we played really well too, as the newspapers of the day recorded. By half-time we were 4–0 ahead through George Best.

We eased a little in the second half and West Ham pulled one back. That spurred us on and we went 5–1 ahead when I converted a penalty and, ten minutes from the end, I smacked the ball into the back of the net to make the final score 6–1. We had a very happy journey back to Manchester knowing that we were League Champions once again.

The following weekend we played our last game of the season. I say 'we' but actually I did not play. I came out at the start and at the end, though, to be presented with the Football League Championship trophy and it was a great feeling to lift it again and show it to our fantastic supporters.

It had been a great season. I don't know which had given me the greater pleasure, winning the title again or playing in the Scotland side which beat England at Wembley a month or so earlier. And there was more good news to come a week and a half later as Celtic won the European Cup. They were the first British side to do it and they were a Scottish team. We would be playing in the European Cup again the following season, and seeing Celtic's great triumph was an inspiration that could not be bettered.

11

KINGS OF EUROPE

Just as 1958 is indelibly marked in the minds of anyone who has ever had any interest in Manchester United, so is 1968 – but for a very different reason. You don't need me to tell you that it was an historic year in which Manchester United finally found the Golden Fleece and became kings of Europe. For me, it was one of the most emotionally mixed-up years that I have ever experienced. On the one hand I was filled with the sheer delight of United's triumph, but on the other I was utterly devastated that injury prevented me from being there on that great night at Wembley when the European Cup was conquered.

The knee injury that I had sustained while playing for Scotland against Poland in October 1965 simply refused to go away. I think there were some at Old Trafford who thought that I was over-emphasizing the problem and that it was no more than a bit of a knock that would eventually sort itself out. That is probably the reason why it took so long for it to be taken seriously enough for some major treatment – which could not have come at a worse time.

In the summer of 1967 we had been taken on an extensive tour to Australia, New Zealand and the United States. It was quite an experience, with perhaps the most daunting moment being when I found myself rubbing noses with a quite large Maori lady. Since our goalkeeper Alex Stepney and I had probably the largest noses in the squad I think we proved to be the most popular, or at least that is what we thought at the time. Believe me, if you have never rubbed noses with a Maori you haven't lived – but don't try it if you have a heavy cold.

By the time the season started properly we had completed our summer tour, had a holiday and drawn 3–3 with Tottenham in the FA Charity Shield. While we were on tour we had been beaten 3–1 by a team that was to become a part of the legend of Manchester United – Benfica. On that tour we met them in Los Angeles. Nobody guessed at that time that the two sides would be lining up against each other less than a year later at Wembley.

The Charity Shield game marked the début of another of United's home-grown players – a teenager by the name of Brian Kidd. Perhaps you have heard of him? The match also became famous for a spectacular goal scored by Tottenham goalkeeper Pat Jennings. He belted the ball up the field with a massive clearance and it went the whole distance – right into our net. I don't know if that has ever happened before or since at Old Trafford but it was certainly one for the record books on that day.

Brian Kidd's League début was on the first day of the season when we played Everton. I remember that he played well but we still lost 1–3, and that put our feet firmly on the ground. Our thoughts were with the European Cup, but we knew that we had a title to defend at home and results like that would not do the trick. We learned our lesson because we then went 11 games without defeat and we particularly enjoyed a 2–1 win at Maine Road against our old rivals.

I had missed a few matches as my knee was giving me trouble again, but I was there when we began our assault on the European Cup with a tie against Hibernian. This was not the Hibernian of Scottish football fame but a team of part-timers from Malta who were coached by a priest. We beat them 4–0 at Old Trafford, with David Sadler and myself getting two goals each. For the return leg in Malta we were told not to overdo things and so we coasted, perhaps a little too much, to a 0–0 draw which gave us a comfortable aggregate victory. It was an amazing tie in more ways than one. Just before the first leg one of the Maltese players went missing. The team had been to watch Arsenal and one of their number, Francis Mifsud, decided to go and buy himself an ice-cream. He did not return. The police were informed and set up a search. He eventually turned up in Manchester and explained that he had become hopelessly lost in London but knew that he was supposed to be playing football in Manchester. A girl had helped him to find his way there. At least, that was the story that he told everyone.

When we arrived in Malta for the return leg we were given a heroes' welcome. I have never seen anything like it on foreign soil. A cavalcade of cars and motorcycles escorted us noisily from the airport to our hotel and along the way we were showered with flowers by what seemed to be the entire population of the island and his dog. I wish that we had given them a better performance during the game but I think they were happy enough to be able to applaud their own men for not losing.

The next round did not take place for a couple of months. In the League we suffered two defeats, at the hands of Nottingham Forest and Leeds, but in general we were doing quite well and certainly enjoyed a 2–1 win over Liverpool at Anfield. For me it was not so good. My knee was now really giving me trouble and I was having to miss matches. At other times I was being patched up to play and I was aware that I was by no means at my best. A six-week suspension for not behaving myself did not help matters either. I had been sent off after a punch-up with Ian Ure, who was with Arsenal at the time. We both had the book thrown at us – and finished up with plenty of time to read it.

I missed the European Cup second round tie against Sarajevo, but was thrilled with the results of the two legs which were a 0–0 draw away and a 2–1 win at home. It was probably just as well that I was not playing in the first leg because everyone said that the Sarajevo tackling was among the worst they had ever encountered. Pat Crerand summed it up when he said that our trainer, Jack Crompton, was on the pitch so often that the crowd thought he was playing. The Yugoslavs proceeded in much the same vein in the return leg and had no reason to complain when they finally had a man sent off.

I came back to the side in early December just in time for the return League game against Everton. We made no mistake this time and beat them 3–1. I scored my third League goal of the season. With the next round of the European Cup not due to take place until February 1968 we were able to concentrate fully on our First Division campaign. The win over Everton set us up for a good Christmas run in which we drew 2-2 with Leicester and then beat Wolves both at home and away. After that we beat West Ham and Sheffield Wednesday and our chances of retaining the championship were looking good.

When we faced Tottenham in the FA Cup third round they held us to a 2–2 draw at Old Trafford and then knocked us out of the competition in the replay with a 1–0 win which I missed because of injury. Nobody wants to miss out on appearing in the FA Cup Final, but sometimes you have to resign yourself to the fact that you are not going to win everything. We did gain some satisfaction a few days after our cup exit because we had to meet Tottenham again in the League and this time we beat them 2–1.

We suffered a set-back when we lost 1–2 at Burnley, but we made up for that by beating Arsenal 2–0 at Highbury in our last League fixture before once again picking up the challenge of winning the European Cup.

We had been drawn against Gornic Zabrze of Poland and were due to face them at home first. It was obvious that the Poles were going to present a harder obstacle than the two teams we had already beaten in the competition that season. They were a tough side who had knocked Celtic out of the European Cup but, unlike Sarajevo, they kept their robust tackling within the rules, apart from an occasional bit of GBH on

George Best. United won 2–0 thanks to an own goal and a neat back flick from Brian Kidd. I'm afraid that I missed both legs of this tie and, though I watched some of the home game, I was in a lot of discomfort because my knee had blown up again and I could hardly stand.

It was a nail-biting second leg. The pitch was covered with snow and like a skating rink underneath, and it is still a mystery why the referee allowed the game to be played, and why he let it continue when the conditions seemed to be getting worse and worse. Still, it ended with a single-goal defeat, which was good enough to earn a place in the semi-finals for Manchester United, so we could hardly complain.

The next European tie was the semi-final and we were drawn to face Real Madrid in what was to be the toughest test thus far. Since we didn't have to worry about that until April we had a further chance to concentrate solely on our League performance. After our victory at Highbury we were three points clear at the top of the table, with Leeds, Liverpool and Manchester City, in that order, beneath us. However, in between the two legs of our European Cup quarter-final, we had suffered two defeats in the First Division and that had not helped our cause at all. We steadied a little by beating Nottingham Forest 3–0, but then came the return derby match with Manchester City, who were now among our chief rivals for the championship.

The game against City was always going to be a bit special but, having beaten them at Maine Road, it was expected that we would do the double over them by winning at Old Trafford. Football is never that simple, though. I did play, but I should not have been on the pitch. City had improved tremendously since our earlier meeting, and we had one or two of our senior players missing. To cut a long story short, they beat us 3–1 and suddenly we had dropped to third place in the table, with Leeds topping it and City second. All three clubs had the same number of points from the same number of games, but Leeds had a superior goal average.

Our form became very patchy after that. We had excellent victories over Stoke City and Fulham, but we lost 1–2 at home to Liverpool at a time when every point was precious. Leeds also faltered a little but City kept on getting the right results and Liverpool also were making a late run. Our last game before we returned to European Cup action was a win at home to Sheffield United. I scored the only goal of the game and once again we were on top of the table. It was exciting stuff if you were a spectator but, for those who were directly involved, the pressure just built and built.

At last we met Real Madrid in the first leg of our semi-final. Only a few days earlier they had been confirmed as Spanish champions again, so they were bursting with confidence when they arrived at Old Trafford. Everyone tells me that it was a great match, with United so dominant that the Spaniards were never able to get into full stride. I remember it as a pretty awful game; I could not get going at all and once again I have to question the good sense in deciding to play me. Perhaps I should feel flattered that I was felt to be necessary, but if I had not been playing, maybe United would have had something more decisive than the 1–0 lead to take to Madrid.

I travelled to Spain for the second leg and it was thought that I would be playing. However, I failed a fitness test, mostly because my temperamental knee had once again decided to inflate itself to twice its normal size. So I had to sit it out and bite my nails as I watched Real Madrid, roared on by their traditionally huge crowd, not only wipe out our single goal lead but race to a 3–1 scoreline before half-time.

In the dressing room there was an air of panic beginning to take a grip, but Matt calmed everyone down as usual and simply reminded his players that the aggregate score was currently only 2–3 in favour of the Spaniards, and that a little more effort could yield a good result. It was a different United that took up the challenge in the second half. There were no more goals until the last 20 minutes and then David Sadler calmly reduced the deficit to 2–3 on the night. More effort was needed, though, and United threw caution to the wind and attacked in wave after wave. Real Madrid could have broken away at any time and put the tie out of reach – but they didn't. They buckled under the strain and had nothing left for an attack of their own. Eventually, in the last couple of minutes, a move seemed to be breaking down the Madrid barrier but the ball went loose. From out of nowhere Bill Foulkes stepped up to meet the loose ball. Just before he made contact I think we were expecting him to hit it into orbit. Instead he surprised us all, and himself probably, by sending in a tremendous long-range shot that fairly smacked into the back of Real's net. The dust had hardly settled from that goal when the referee blew his whistle to end the game and Manchester United were, at last, in the final of the European Cup.

Much had happened on the League scene in between those two semi-final games. We went to West Bromwich three days after the first leg. They had reached the final of the FA Cup and had nothing to win or lose in the First Division, so we were not expecting them to turn it on against us. We were very wrong. We often underestimated just how much other clubs wanted to beat Manchester United. West Brom gave us a hiding and we journeyed home with a 3–6 scoreline hanging round our necks. We also heard that Manchester City had beaten Everton 2–0 and gone top of the table for the first time, so it was a sombre return journey to Manchester.

For me there was worse news. Once again my knee had caused me all sorts of problems and I suspected that I would not be playing again that season. Nothing was definite but I sensed that, even if we did reach the European Cup Final, it would be touch and go whether I would appear.

With two games to go to end the First Division season, anything could happen. The advantage was with Manchester City but it was not over yet. George Best scored a brilliant hat-trick, Brian Kidd got a couple and David Sadler scored one as Newcastle were beaten 6–0. United were not going to give up the championship without fighting to the end. Everything hinged on the results of the last day of the season and the north-east was heavily involved because United were at home to Sunderland while City had to travel to Newcastle. It proved to be a big anti-climax because not only did City win 4–2 at St James's Park, but United lost 1–2 at Old Trafford. It was very frustrating because at the final count Manchester United had finished in second place – just two points behind Manchester City. We had lost the championship by a whisker, and to our rivals across the city. It was typical of Matt Busby that he immediately sent them a message of congratulation.

This is probably an appropriate time for a 'knees bulletin'. As you will have gathered, my knee was up and down more times than a bouncy castle during the season, and I was not entirely happy with the treatment I had received. I knew that there was more to the problem than something that could be fixed with a pain-killing injection or a poultice. It became a bit of a beef with me because I felt that professional players were being sent into battle without being fully fit, and with little regard for the long-term effects. I did not blame Manchester United in particular for that. It was just the way that things were done in football then and I'm afraid that, despite all the modern techniques and equipment, it is much the same today.

My season had been ruined by being constantly in and out of the side because of the knee trouble. I know that countless other players have had the same problem. There is always pressure on you to play and on managers to send you out to perform. Probably all that pressure has intensified to match the transfer fees that have escalated so astronomically. It was bad enough when I was playing but today, when clubs spend millions and millions on an individual player, the last thing they want to see is him sidelined with a dodgy ankle or knee. Quite often they will find a short-term answer to the problem by giving him a pain-killer. The fact that this means the injury does not get any better until it eventually has to be rested for a couple of months, instead of the week or so that would originally have done the trick, does not seem to enter into the

145

equation. Worse still is the fact that the player may well be unable to walk properly when he gets older.

I had umpteen cortisone injections, various poultices, visits to supposed experts, and so on. I tried my best, and even put away my golf clubs for six years in case golf was adding to the problem. I regularly felt a sharp, stabbing pain inside my knee and it would often catch me out during matches. I tried running freezing cold water on the knee for long periods at a time and I can honestly say that, throughout the 1967–68 season, I spent more time in our bathroom than in any other room of the house. It had become my own personal medical room and I was sick of the sight of it. I was acquainted with every tile in the place and I was beginning to call the bath-taps by their first names. Yes, all right, it was driving me crazy.

After our FA Cup defeat by Tottenham, Matt arranged for me to go and see a Harley Street specialist. I had been to so-called specialists before and had got no nearer to solving the problem, but this one was different. He became Sir Osmond-Clarke, but when I consulted him he was a plain Mister. He really knew his stuff and his conclusions were frightening. The bottom line was that my career was in serious jeopardy. That worried me. I was not quite 28 years old and I had no thoughts of ending my career for some years to come. He warned me that if I did not take out the time for proper surgery and recovery, I might as well say goodbye to playing football at the top level. He gave me no more than one more season at the top if I did not have firstly exploratory and then remedial surgery. He also pointed out that even that might achieve nothing more than prolonging my football life for a little while. He felt that the damage to my knee was beyond repair, but that there was a chance it could be patched up sufficiently for me to see out the rest of my playing career.

Following that consultation the club decided that I should carry on training for four weeks and have Faradism treatment to see what would happen. After that the situation would be looked at again to check if there had been any improvement.

146

During that time I again had a lot of pain from my knee and, to ease the agony, I was given a Protocain injection, which I had never had before. Later I wished the stuff had never been invented.

I went home to rest before returning to Old Trafford for a game that evening, but instead I became very ill. My family were all away, so I was in the house on my own. I managed to get out of bed but found that I couldn't walk and I had to crawl head-first down the stairs to reach the telephone and summon help. It turned out that I was allergic to Protocain. That was all I needed. I was admitted to hospital where I had a huge amount of fluid drained from my knee. I could feel it going and soon felt much better – but apparently it had been touch and go and, if I hadn't managed to reach that telephone, anything could have happened.

Not too long after that I took the law into my own hands when I was recommended to go and visit a gentleman by the name of Millwood. He was an osteopath, which, to me, was some kind of a witch-doctor. Yes, I admit I was ignorant. I was prepared to try anything and so I went along to see him. He manipulated my knee joint and it did bring me some relief. I was so impressed that I continued visiting him for years afterwards every time I had a knock. He could not cure the problem but I always felt a whole lot better after his treatment than I had ever done from most of the others I had received. I broke a club rule by sorting out my own treatment and I was given a ticking-off when it was discovered. I retaliated by saying that I felt it was doing me much more good than all the previous efforts and I intended to carry on whether Manchester United liked it or not. They didn't like it, but there was not much they could do because I was quite determined.

At long last it was decided that I should have the surgery suggested by Mr Osmond-Clarke, and Matt thought it would be best if I went into hospital immediately after going to Wembley to watch the European Cup Final. I appreciated the gesture but I wanted to get it over with and, since there was no chance of me doing anything other than watch the game, I thought it would be better if I went into hospital at the earliest opportunity to give myself a longer recovery time to prepare for the following season.

And that is how I came to be in hospital and watching television along with millions of other people as my club and my team-mates experienced their greatest moment in defeating Benfica at Wembley to win the European Cup. What a night it was – and what a massive disappointment not to have been there. If only my knee had been taken more seriously months earlier, I might well have been playing in that match.

Anyway, by the time the final took place I had mostly recovered from my disappointment and I sat there in the hospital cheering on my pals. A few times I had to be reminded not to get too excited. But, as I watched Bobby, George and the others playing out of their skins to win that trophy, and then seeing the tears in Matt's eyes as he finally took hold of it – the trophy that he had always wanted – how could I possibly sit there just passively observing? No way! I was leaping up and down cheering, waving my arms about and laughing along with millions of other TV viewers. My club – Manchester United – had just become Kings of Europe.

12

END OF AN ERA

With the European Cup won and handed over by the then UEFA President, Gustav Wiederkehr, I could well understand the tears of the boss and of Bobby Charlton, who had been through hell together in pursuit of that elusive trophy. Matt was as eloquent as ever in talking to the press about that great triumph but he maintained an edge of steel when he said, 'This is not the end of something, it is just the beginning.' He was both right and wrong.

Since that brilliant night in May, Manchester United have been in search of repeating that success, so Matt was right when he said that it was just a beginning. In the 30 or so years since then United have grown bigger and bigger and there have been many causes for the team, some lost and some achieved. On the other hand he was wrong because it was the end of something, and he was the focal point of that termination.

When I emerged from hospital clutching a jar containing all the rubbish that had been removed from my knee, I could not wait to get back into action. I knew that I had missed out on the big prize and that, had I been fit, it would probably have been me leading the team up to receive the trophy and the medals. I was not bitter about that, but I did want to get on with the job of trying to help United repeat the performance.

There was a further boost for the club when the news broke,

a few weeks after the European Cup Final, that Matt was to become Sir Matt Busby. He thoroughly deserved the honour and I was very pleased for him.

The trouble with winning a major trophy is that everyone is even keener to beat you, and none were keener than Estudiantes, the Argentinian side that we were to play against in the World Club Cup match that pitched the champions of Europe against the champions of South America. There was a time when we thought that the match would not go ahead. Celtic had experienced a nightmare game against Racing Club the previous year and had stated that, if they won the European Cup again, there was no way they would play another South American club to decide who was best in the world. The boss had the final word and decided that it was doubtful that Celtic's dreadful experience would be repeated. The first leg in Argentina was scheduled for late September, so there was a chance for us to get into match routine before making the trip.

It was good to report back for pre-season training and I worked extra hard to prove my fitness, both to myself and to the management. Once again we were to play Everton in the opening game of the season and this time the pendulum swung in our favour and we won 2–1. When we looked ahead to the fixtures for the next month or so, it was a daunting prospect. In the seven weeks until the end of September we would have to complete ten First Division matches, a European Cup first leg tie and the first leg of the World Club Championship, which involved travelling to Argentina. It was exhausting just to think about it. They say that there are too many games today, and they are most certainly right, but it is not a new problem by any means.

We won four of those ten opening League matches, but we also lost four, including a 4–5 defeat at Sheffield Wednesday which was a thriller to say the least. I had played in six and scored four goals, which was quite encouraging, considering that I had only scored seven League goals in all of the previous season. I also scored a hat-trick as we beat Waterford 3–1 in our opening European Cup tie. Before the return leg, and immediately after we had beaten Newcastle 3–0 in the League, we boarded the plane that took us to Argentina.

It was a bit like going to the OK Corral for a shoot-out. We were the first English team to visit Argentina since the 1966 World Cup and Sir Alf Ramsey's famous comment about the Argentine national side being 'animals'. Everyone was very charming when we arrived but the press were already whipping up anti-United feeling and, in particular, they picked on Nobby Stiles and called him all sorts of names, including 'The Assassin'. If you knew Nobby you would know what a joke that was. He was a hard little devil and, like myself, he would not take any nonsense from people, but he was never the cynical destruction machine that he had been painted.

The charm with which we had been met soon evaporated and gave way to bad feeling. Gamesmanship was the order of the day and, as we tried to acclimatize ourselves and adjust our body clocks after the marathon journey, we were constantly disturbed for one reason or another. The worst was when we were invited to a reception in Buenos Aires to meet our opponents for the first time. We gave up valuable relaxation time to go along to that function, though our hotel was about an hour and a half away by coach, since it was felt that our attendance would be good for public relations. To cut a long story short, Estudiantes never turned up and nobody at the reception seemed surprised except us. We came away fairly certain that it had all been an elaborate ploy to lose us about six hours of valuable preparation time.

If the pre-match gamesmanship had been annoying, what happened during the game was downright disgusting. We played at the Boca Juniors Stadium in Buenos Aires, filled to capacity with hostile supporters. It would have taken a referee with no sense of self-preservation to officiate properly and, unfortunately, ours had very astutely decided that he did not wish to spend time in the local hospital after the game.

In the first minute I went for the ball only to be held back – by my hair. My marker, an apprentice dentist, decided to introduce himself by trying to extract my top teeth by tugging at my hair-roots. I was wide-eyed – partly through disbelief and partly through being half-scalped. Any more of that, pal, and it'll be me taking the teeth out in the Scottish way, I thought. That set the tone for the game as Estudiantes seemed to be going all out to carve notches on our legs or collect blood samples. We could not believe what was happening, but Matt had drummed into us that we shouldn't get involved, so we just gritted our teeth and put up with it. It was not just the so-called tackles, elbows and punches, there was also a lot of spitting and a little trick they must have learned from the Spanish Inquisition: their idea of a sporting gesture was to help you up and pinch your armpits at the same time.

Nobby Stiles had his head split open when one of our hosts head-butted him and then fell to the ground as if the assault had been the other way about. The referee was going to send Nobby off when he saw the blood and couldn't make up his mind as to what had happened. A few minutes later, though, Nobby did get his marching orders as he protested to the referee when a linesman turned a blind eye to a blatant Estudiantes off-side. Nobby said a few words and made a rude gesture and off he went. I wish I had done that in the very first minute.

The result seems almost irrelevant but we lost 0–1. Nobby had to have stitches in his head wound, Bobby Charlton needed stitches in a gash etched into his leg, and the rest of us were carrying multi-coloured bruises. Matt was furious about the refereeing but congratulated us for not completely losing our tempers. I remember him saying that if you lose your heads you lose the match. Well, we lost the match, our heads got a battering but we didn't actually lose them, and the one thing that we did was keep our dignity.

Sir Stanley Rous, the President of FIFA, who was at the game, said, 'The most outstanding feature of it all was the

Di often helps me with the housework.

Why do goalkeepers do things like this?

Come and get it then, if you can.

This is the earliest 'early bath' ever.

Joining City for the second time.

Good tackle, but *I* came away with the ball.

Celebrating with Billy after qualifying for the 1973 World Cup.

Two fine figures of men – training with Bestie.

Just after scoring *that* goal against United.

Lining up with the Rest of the World side at Wembley.

Rod Stewart copied my style. One of my last games ever – City v Liverpool.

(Manchester Evening News)

Straight from the family album.

The joy of becoming a dad.
Now I am the family chauffeur.

They even pinched my caps!

A mad Scotsman on his way to Argentina to commentate on the 1978 World Cup.

Fans get my autograph during the 1978 World Cup.

(©Colorsport)

A reunion of former European Players of the Year.

This is where I lived as a boy. It rained then as well.

Bestie, Matt, Bobby and yours truly. Magic!

tolerance of Manchester United. We can all be proud of them.' That statement genuinely made us feel a lot better, but there is no telling what we would like to have done had we met them up a dark alley in the back-streets of Buenos Aires.

We arrived in England just in time for our return European Cup leg with Waterford, and that game gently eased us back into civilization. I scored four goals as we won 7–1 and went through to the next round with a 10–2 aggregate. At the end of the match we warmly shook the hands of those Irishmen. They were a breath of fresh air after our trip to Argentina.

Drawn League matches against Arsenal and Tottenham, and a defeat by Liverpool which I missed, did not exactly help us as we prepared to face the dreaded Estudiantes for the second leg at Old Trafford. This time we were at least going to be among friends, but we were still not looking forward to meeting the Argentinians again. We were not afraid of them, but it all seemed so pointless. We were on a hiding to nothing because there seemed little sense in trying to win a fairly meaningless competition when your opponents are only interested in seeing what colour your bones are.

Estudiantes toned down their attack for the visit to Old Trafford, but not by very much. I had to go off because their goalkeeper wanted to create a deep impression on my shin. His metal studs raked down my leg and I had to have stitches. Besty finally lost it with the guy who had been trying to maim him in both games and they were both sent off for fighting. It ended 1–1, which meant that the Argentinians won the trophy. We were just glad that it was over and the club announced that it would be following Celtic's example in refusing to take part in the competition again should they qualify by winning the European Cup.

Sir Alf Ramsey's description of the Argentinians as 'animals' kept coming into my mind and for once I found myself agreeing with him. I have had some pretty rough games in various competitions but those two legs were the worst footballing experiences that I have ever endured. During the following few years both Ajax and AC Milan had the same problem, which proved that it was not just British clubs who were suffering at the hands of the South Americans. It still makes me shudder when I think about it and I don't believe I have ever been accused of cowardice.

Our League results lacked consistency again and we even hit a patch of finding it difficult to score goals. In November 1968 we played four drawn games on the trot and only scored once. I missed a few matches through various injuries but I was encouraged by the fact that I was scoring again fairly frequently. When we played Anderlecht in the next round of the European Cup I was delighted to set up a new United scoring record, taking my tally to 14 in that competition as I scored twice against our visitors from Belgium. I cannot deny that I would have created the new record quicker if I had not failed with penalties against both Anderlecht and Waterford. We won the first leg 3–0 but we had a scare in the second when we conceded three goals. Carlo Sartori scored for us, though, and the aggregate was 4–3 in our favour, which was just enough to squeeze us into the quarter-finals.

Apart from a 1–0 home victory against Liverpool, our December 1968 programme was dismal. We lost to Leicester, Southampton and Arsenal. By the end of the year we were in the First Division relegation zone, and genuinely wished each other a Happy New Year as we looked for a change in our fortunes in 1969.

The new year began with a hard-won 3–1 FA Cup victory at Exeter. We were helped by an own goal, which was just as well because Exeter had given us a scare. A week later we lost a First Division game at Leeds, who were going strong at the time and did, eventually, go on to win the League Championship. It had been a less than stimulating start to 1969, but there was worse to come.

It was on 14 January that the press were summoned to a news conference in the players' lounge at Old Trafford. They guessed that Matt was going into the transfer market to find a cure for our ailing League form. They were shocked, therefore, when it was announced that Matt would be retiring at the end of that season. It was a total shock to all of us. We knew he wasn't getting any younger and we were aware he had some health problems, which was not surprising when you remember everything he had been through, but we were not expecting such a dramatic announcement.

As a player you try not to allow speculation to get to you but, in such a situation as we found ourselves, we could not help but wonder who was going to be appointed to try and fill Matt's shoes. We were relieved that the boss was still going to be around, even though we knew that his new role as general manager would not involve him in team affairs. It was of great concern to us who would be our new boss. I think the older players, like myself, were especially worried because we felt we had a good few years left and did not want to find ourselves on the scrap heap just because a new face wanted to make major changes to try and prove something.

Old Trafford was full once again a few days later when we played at home to Sunderland in the First Division. We decided that we would do our best for the boss to show him how we felt about his announcement. We won 4–0. Best scored one and I got a hat-trick. My next hat-trick that season came in the FA Cup. We beat Watford after a replay in the fourth round and then drew away to Birmingham in the fifth round. In the replay at Old Trafford we beat them 6–2 and that set us up for the first leg of our European Cup quarter-final against Rapid Vienna at Old Trafford.

The Austrians put up a good fight but we beat them 3–0 at home and then drew 0–0 away to book our place in the semi-finals for the second successive season. We came out of the hat against AC Milan but, since the ties were not until April, we had the opportunity to do something about our precarious League position. Our first game in March was against Everton in the FA Cup sixth round and they beat us 1–0 at Old Trafford, so that put an end to our aspirations in that competition. We then lost the derby game at home to Manchester City by the only goal of the match and followed that with a 0–0 draw at Everton, and then a 2–3 defeat at Chelsea. Our position in the table was looking dire – sixth from the bottom and by no means safe from relegation.

In all fairness, we had experienced nothing but trouble from bad injuries during that season. I had been in and out of the side, Bobby Charlton lost nine weeks through a knee ligament injury, John Aston had broken his leg in the first month of the campaign, Nobby Stiles and Francis Burns were suffering from cartilage problems, Tony Dunne had a broken jaw and there were numerous minor niggles which had prevented us from putting out our strongest side on a regular basis. No excuses, though. We knew we had to get our act together or we could be in serious danger of becoming the first European Cup holders to be relegated.

That is why Queens Park Rangers received such a beating when they visited Old Trafford in the middle of March 1969. Willie Morgan had settled in well since joining us in September and he hit his first hat-trick for United as we hammered QPR 8–1. That gave us a lift and we went on a run of seven games without defeat which made all the difference. Apart from defeats at Coventry and Newcastle we did not lose again during that League season and our position strengthened to a more respectable 11th place.

At the end of April we travelled to Italy for the first leg of our European Cup semi-final against AC Milan. We lost Nobby Stiles during the game when his suspect knee locked and he had to be carried off. The home side always had the benefit of the doubt in any decisions and, at the end of 90 minutes, they had won 2–0. We knew they would put up a typically rigid defensive wall for the return leg and that it would be difficult for us to break it down, but we were still optimistic we could reach the final. We had forgotten about the ethics, or lack of them, of some referees and I honestly believe that we were robbed by some diabolical decisions. At Torino, one of my pals had been Roberto Rosato, but he now played for Milan and had the job of keeping me under control, so there was no old pals act. I did talk to him during the match to calm him down as his tackling was getting more and more dangerous. In the end I smacked him one when the referee was distracted and that seemed to get through to him. I got away with it for once, too.

As for the 'robbery', Bobby Charlton found the net for us to make it 1–2 on aggregate and, seven minutes later, I 'scored'. There was no doubt in my mind or anyone else's that the ball not only went over the line but cleared it by at least a foot. However, an Italian boot kicked it away and the referee waved play on. It was just incredible. The French referee was only a few yards from the ball and had an unobstructed view. He must have seen that it was over the line and yet he refused what would have been the equalizer. There has been much talk over the years about certain clubs 'buying the favours' of officials, and AC Milan have been in trouble with the authorities several times for offering 'gifts' to referees and linesmen. I am not alleging that that particular referee on that particular night was wearing a Milan badge, but it certainly makes you think, especially since photographic and television evidence has since proved, without the shadow of a doubt, that the ball was indeed well over the line and that we had in fact equalized.

I don't like to speculate on what might have been, but I do feel that we would most likely have gone on to beat Milan that night and, since they eventually won the European Cup by beating Ajax 4–1 in the final, I think there was a very good chance that we would have retained the Cup but for that terrible refereeing decision.

Our last match of the season was our final First Division fixture against Leicester City at Old Trafford. We desperately wanted to win because it was a fitting way to say farewell to Sir Matt Busby. Our visitors did not make it easy for us but we still ran out 3–2 winners, and I'm happy to say that, as well as Willie Morgan's and George Best's, my name went on the scoresheet.

We had won nothing that season but I was glad to have landed back among the top scorers. Besty beat me in the League but, overall, I was the club's top scorer in major competitions with 30 goals.

All that paled into insignificance, though, compared with the fact that we were no longer going to have Matt in charge. A few weeks before the end of the season the speculation had finally ended when Wilf McGuinness was named as the new chief coach. Wilf had been at Old Trafford all his life as a player and a coach. His playing days had ended prematurely because of injury but he had been given coaching work with the youth and reserves squads, and had also become involved with the England set-up, so he was not short of a few ideas. However, I felt uneasy at the decision because he was only 31 and I did not feel he had sufficient experience to take on such a massive job. He might have been labelled chief coach but that was as near to being called manager as anyone could get. I hoped my fears would prove to be wrong.

It was good to bump into Matt regularly at Old Trafford after that, but I don't think he was ever quite the same after resigning his post. I had known him for many years as man and boy, and we had crossed swords now and then too, but he had always been big enough to talk things out with me and I had tremendous respect for him. He had been the driving force of Manchester United for as long as I could remember. He had endured the tragedy and wounds of Munich. He had built three great teams. He had won championships, the FA Cup and the mighty European Cup.

Matt had been both general and father to his players. He had yelled at them when necessary, cried with them, laughed with them, made examples of them, praised them, loaned money to them, engulfed them within his family circle, and helped them with their futures once they had left the Old Trafford nest. He had succeeded in being all things to all people.

To this day Manchester United are still the 'Busby Boys' but, when the final whistle blew on 17 May 1969 and we had beaten

Leicester 3–2, Matt stood and returned the applause of the adoring supporters before turning to disappear into the board-room. His face was still to be seen at Old Trafford for many years to come but somehow, as we watched him turn away from his seat, we all knew that we were witnessing the end of an era.

13

DROPPED

I had a new experience under Wilf McGuinness. For the first time in my career I was dropped. I wasn't the only one; Bobby Charlton suffered the same fate. It came as a shock to both of us, but our shock was nothing compared to the ripples that went out of Old Trafford and even made news around the world. I didn't blame Wilf for what he did. He was the boss with a job to protect and he had to stand or fall by his decisions, so it was up to him to do what he thought was best for Manchester United. I did not necessarily agree with him but I respected that it was his decision to make.

Things had not seemed quite the same when we reported back for training before the 1969–70 season. I have already said that I did not think that Wilf McGuinness was experienced enough. Jimmy Murphy was not considered because he was thought to be too old, and I believe that the club made a mistake in that respect. If Jimmy had done a couple of seasons with Wilf as his number two, the outcome might have been a lot better. I thought so at the time, so I am not just being clever with the benefit of hindsight.

The new campaign began with a 2–2 draw at Crystal Palace but I think it was the following game, our first home match against Everton, which put the writing on the wall. We lost 0–2 and a few days later lost at home again, this time to Southampton who gave us a 4–1 beating. Each of the

Southampton goals was headed home by Ron Davies, their Welsh international centre-forward, and that meant that there was something very wrong in our defence. We had to play away to Everton in our next match and the chief coach decided to make a number of changes. That is how it came to pass that Bobby and myself were dropped, along with Jimmy Rimmer, our goalkeeper, Bill Foulkes and Tony Dunne. Almost half the team found themselves sidelined. The result was a 0–3 defeat.

By the next game, Bobby and I were back and Ian Ure had been signed from Arsenal to replace Bill Foulkes, who had played his last game for Manchester United. We drew 0–0 at Wolverhampton but I did not last the full 90 minutes. I turned awkwardly, injured my groin and had to be replaced. That was to keep me out of the side for more than two months. During that time United did pull in some better results and suffered only two defeats in their next 12 League matches. Despite my injuries I was still involved in first-team matters and I noticed that Wilf McGuinness was doing his best to stamp his authority on Manchester United.

Matt Busby had always given us the licence to go out and show what we could do. He had only the slightest of game plans and expected us as professionals to have the sense and ability to deal with the various aspects of each match during the playing time itself. McGuinness was much different. He was a blackboard manager who liked to spend ages explaining moves and tactics. To be honest, we were usually quite baffled by the time he had finished each session. We used to nod our heads at the right times, but these robotic plans meant very little to us. We did try to put into practice the things that he wanted, but they veered towards defensive football and we had always been an attacking side. Players like Pat Crerand, who were renowned for their ability to create scoring chances, were now expected to spend their game back-pedalling. It was like trying to make a bacon sandwich with two biscuits and a banana.

Despite that, the side strung some good results together and, when I returned to the first team on 1 November 1969, we drew with Stoke and then beat Coventry 2–1. The game after that was a total disaster, however. We had the first of several meetings that season with Manchester City and they beat us 4–0. That was really bad news. I then missed the next few games, which included another match at Maine Road, this time in the semi-final first leg of the League Cup. Once again City were the victors, winning 2–1, but their winner was a hotly disputed penalty in the last minute.

The game became famous for an incident which happened as the teams left the pitch. George Best had a few words with the referee, Jack Taylor, and playfully knocked the ball out of his hand. He was suspended for a month for that. It is just another indication of how much the game has changed. Nowadays I cannot believe what I see players getting away with. They hurl abuse at referees, use threatening body language and jostle them, but rarely does a referee take any action. It leaves me speechless at times – and for something to render me speechless it has to be very remarkable.

I was back for the second leg of that tie and scored as we drew 2–2, but City went through to the final on aggregate. We played City again later in the season, in the return League fixture at Old Trafford, and they beat us yet again. This time it was a 1–2 result, but we gained some satisfaction by knocking them out of the FA Cup when we beat them 3–0 in our fourth round tie at Old Trafford. I think that win just about kept our chins off the floor in Manchester.

We had a bit of a run in the FA Cup again, with probably the most famous match being the 8–2 win away to Northampton in which Besty scored an amazing six goals. It was his first game back after suspension and he was determined to turn it on a bit. He actually turned it on a lot, but I think he only wanted to score six goals in a cup tie because I had done it several years earlier. The difference was that his counted. We reached the semi-finals, where we had to face Leeds at Hillsborough. It was a 0–0 draw, which was not a great surprise because in both League meetings between the two sides that season the result had been 2–2. The replay was at Villa Park and once again the result was a 0–0 draw. I was substitute and replaced Carlo Sartori, as I did in the second replay at Burnden Park. This time Leeds won 1–0 when Billy Bremner let fly with a 35-yarder late in the game and it proved to be the tie-breaker.

For most of the season we were around the middle of the table but a few particularly good results, like the 4–1 win away against Liverpool and the 7–0 home defeat of West Bromwich, pushed us up into eighth place at the season's close. Ironically, Manchester City finished several places below us while Everton, who had given us so much trouble at the start of the season, were crowned champions.

On paper we had improved our League standing but in fact there was little in it and, despite the more defensive approach by McGuinness, we had conceded more goals than in the previous season. We were out of sorts and we knew it. I was quite fed up because I had made only ten appearances and scored two goals in the League, and in the two major cups I had played only five times in 17 games, two of them as substitute. I had scored three goals in the cups, which took my total to five for the entire season, my worst season since the early days of my career.

There was worse in store. I had come face to face with the realization that I would no longer be given the benefit of the doubt if I had a poor game. That was fair enough, although I don't think that allowance was made for the new tactics which did not suit my game at all. Nor must it be forgotten that you can go through the pain barrier with injuries only for so long before you start to get a little slower during the 90 minutes.

What came as a total surprise was being placed on the transfer list. It was decided that I was no longer wanted at Old Trafford. Again it was not just me because Shay Brennan was also surplus to requirements. I was never quite sure whether it was decided to let me go because I had not had the best of seasons or because I was one of those guys who liked to say his piece. It has always been my policy that if you have something to say you should say it, and not let things fester in your mind. Not everyone appreciates that of course, and I was often considered the loudest of the raised voices in the United dressing room. And there had been raised voices that season, with some players even going to discuss things with Matt, who did his best to keep away from team affairs but never closed his door to anyone who needed to talk.

Not only was I placed on the transfer list but a price-tag of £60,000 was put on me. I had been at Old Trafford for eight successful seasons but it seemed that I was now considered to be of no further use – yet the price asked was quite high for someone being written off. I could not understand that and it did not surprise me that the telephone remained silent. No manager in his right mind would be prepared to pay that sort of money for a player who couldn't do it any more.

I set about putting matters straight. The World Cup was taking place in Mexico, so the season had ended a couple of weeks earlier. That gave me the chance to really work on my health and fitness, so throughout that summer I trained and trained. I had treatment to make sure that my limbs and my groin were in as good a condition as possible before we reported back, and I went to the gym six days a week. By the time we all assembled at Old Trafford once again to prepare for the new season I was feeling super-fit and left a lot of the younger players standing as we trained.

Talk of my transfer went off the agenda and life continued as before. The only real change was that Wilf McGuinness had gone from being chief coach to manager, a move which meant very little to any of us because we had considered that to be his role from the start.

I did not play in the first two games of the 1970–71 season. They were both at home and resulted in a 0–1 defeat by Leeds and a 0–0 draw with Chelsea. The first away fixture was a trip to Arsenal where we were well beaten 4–0. I did play in that one but we were never truly in the match and Arsenal soon sorted out our defensive plan. Things were much better when we travelled to Burnley because we won 2–0. It was our first victory of the season and I scored both goals, which meant that I had at least equalled the previous season's League goal tally.

We put a few good results together following that until Ipswich beat us 4–0 at Portman Road. From then on we were struggling. The atmosphere in the dressing room worsened. The players became increasingly confused by the deluge of tactics and frustration began to set in. During the reign of the previous manager any raised voices were quickly calmed, but I don't think Wilf had the experience to deal with such situations and nothing was resolved. This was not a good time for Manchester United. By the middle of December we had won just five of our 20 First Division games. In fairness we had progressed to the semi-finals of the League Cup, but that was going to be yet another disaster as we were knocked out by Aston Villa, who were then a Third Division side.

Before playing Villa we had the first derby of the season at Old Trafford. There was a great determination to beat Manchester City in front of our own supporters but once again it was a big let-down. They beat us 4–1 and I was substituted by Carlo Sartori. A week later Arsenal visited Old Trafford and they took the points with a 3–1 win. By the time we had been knocked out of the League Cup, the season was beginning to look a real mess. Nothing was going right and there was a great deal of speculation about Wilf McGuinness losing his job.

The board rubbished the idea that Wilf would be going and we all wondered what the second half of the season would be like. We were already about fifth from bottom and it seemed that the threat of relegation could only get greater. On Boxing Day I returned to the side and scored twice as we managed a 4–4 draw at Derby County. That was much more like it, but it proved to be too little too late for our manager.

After a meeting on 28 December, the directors of the club decided that something dramatic had to be done to prevent the unthinkable from taking place. Wilf McGuinness relinquished his post as manager and went back to looking after the reserves. The new man was a very familiar face to us. In fact we didn't have to see him walking through the door to recognize him – the pipe smoke was a dead giveaway. Sir Matt had agreed to take charge once again, but only until the end of the season.

His first game back was the third round of the FA Cup at home to Middlesbrough, in which we got a draw, then losing in the replay. That didn't really matter to us much. We knew the real task was to preserve our status as a First Division club. The atmosphere in the dressing room changed completely and we all felt we were going to play real football again.

Our first League match following the return of Sir Matt as manager was away to Chelsea. We were well aware that it was not going to be an easy trip. However, our confidence and our spirit had been so completely changed that it was almost like the start of a new season for us and we won 2–1. It was the signal for our fight-back. We dropped a point at home to Burnley in our next match but then won three games in succession, including a 5–1 victory over Southampton. We gradually began to climb the table and our theme tune could easily have become 'Happy Days Are Here Again'.

Although we did suffer a few defeats in the second half of the season, we never again had the same feeling of despair and frustration that had been so dominant in our dressing room earlier in the campaign. Our climb up the table continued and, when I hit a hat-trick in our 5–3 victory at Crystal Palace, it was as if someone had turned the clock back. Bobby Charlton was enjoying his football again and George Best was back to his brilliant best. At the end of the season we had reached eighth place and I was our second top scorer with 15 goals from 28 League appearances. George beat me with three goals more from 12 more appearances. I have since forgiven him.

The last match of the season was away to Manchester City and we had a big score to settle. We also guessed that it was going to be Sir Matt's last game in charge because we knew that the club would have to appoint a new manager at some time and therefore next season we would almost certainly be playing for the new man.

It turned out to be probably one of the best derby games ever seen in Manchester. From the moment he took over, the boss had told us that we were to forget all the blackboard stuff and concentrate on playing football the way we always had when he was in charge. He stressed that once again we had the freedom to go out and enjoy ourselves and play as top professionals should. He urged us to attack. It was music to our ears and, since we had gone from 18th to eighth place, we wished that we had been allowed to play this way from the start. We were convinced that, if we had, we would have been champions.

As if to remind everyone of what football was about, Sir Matt selected a five-man forward line for the trip to Maine Road on the last day of that season. He went for all-out attack and let the defence look after itself. Matt never liked to give away goals, but he maintained that if you scored two it did not matter if you let in one. If you conceded nine then you had to score ten.

Well, at Maine Road that day, Manchester City put three past us, which was one fewer than they had managed at Old Trafford back in the previous December. We were not dismayed. Far from it, in fact. Because we scored four. Besty hit two, Bobby scored one and I got the other. So the old Charlton–Law–Best trio was in full working order.

The supporters had quite a knees-up on the terraces. We had gained revenge over the enemy, we had avoided relegation with a second half of the season display that was worthy of trophy-winners, and we had enjoyed Sir Matt Busby being back in charge of things again. I had my own little celebration too. All that work the previous summer had done the trick, so that when my old boss had taken over again I was up to the standard he required. Now there was no longer any talk of my name going on to the transfer list, and that made me very happy.

I felt a bit sorry for Wilf McGuinness. I had said all along that he had been thrown in at the deep end and was just not up to the job at that stage in his career. There is little time for sentiment in football and it was the right decision to replace him rather than to allow the situation to get worse. Sir Matt's presence in the dressing room had given all of us a new lease of life and had been the saving of Manchester United.

As we went our separate ways for the summer, we knew that the boss had once again slipped into retirement and that this time it was going to be for good. He did not return to being general manager but became a director instead. Of course, the question on everyone's lips was, and had been for some months, who was going to be the new manager. Jock Stein, Dave Sexton, Don Revie and Don Howe were among the names being earnestly promoted by the press but, in reality, every one of us was in the dark. So, who would the new manager be? And, as it turned out, would anyone notice?

14

THE INVISIBLE MANAGER

You might not think that it would be possible to have an invisible manager at a football club, but we did at Manchester United after Sir Matt finally hung up his pipe for the second time. He had saved us from going down, there is no question of that in my mind, and the season had ended on quite a respectable note when earlier it had seemed inevitable that it would end in total shame. We were eager to find out who the new boss would be but, when we finally learned that the man of the moment was going to be Frank O'Farrell, the dressing room was filled with a resounding silence.

Don't get me wrong. We had nothing at all against Frank. He had performed something of a mini-miracle at Leicester by establishing them as a very useful side without spending a great deal of money. Actually he had no money to spend and so it had been a case of do-or-die for him at Filbert Street, and he had certainly not 'died'. Matt was involved in the talks with Frank O'Farrell and was there at the press conference when he was introduced. From 1 July 1971, Frank O'Farrell was our boss with Malcolm Musgrove making the move with him from Leicester as his second in command.

It was another new beginning for Manchester United. O'Farrell was older and more experienced than Wilf McGuinness and we hoped that this quiet Irishman would be the ideal replacement for Sir Matt. I can even remember

Besty saying that he thought United had made a wise choice. The reason why we were so silent and noncommittal about his appointment was the fact that none of us knew him. Even those who had had some contact with him before said that they did not really know him. None of us knew just what to expect. We were all prepared to give him our best shot, though.

Pre-season training soon gave us some indication of what we could expect. Training was under the supervision of Malcolm Musgrove, whom I found to be quite good, and I got on pretty well with him. We were not subjected to sitting in front of a blackboard for hours on end but we did seem to spend an awful lot of time on set-pieces on the training ground. It was also a little bit like being back at school because we were continually being directed by the whistle. However, apart from that, our training sessions were for the most part quite enjoyable. The only thing missing was the manager. Frank used to be at the Cliff every day, but we hardly ever saw him. He would rush into his office as soon as he arrived and never come out except for the Friday team talk. I often imagined that he had barricaded himself in and was sitting under his desk in case anyone wanted to ask him something. Of course it wasn't anything like that but it used to amuse me to think about it. I also got to wondering if he perhaps had a secret potion which he drank to make him invisible, and that he was actually out there on the training ground with us. If he was, it was he who tripped me up once or twice.

We did not play at Old Trafford until our seventh game of the 1971–72 campaign. There had been a crowd problem the previous season and some lunatic had thrown a knife on to the pitch. As a result we had to play our first two home games on neutral grounds that were at least 25 miles away. First of all, we had two genuine away matches, which were a 2–2 draw at Derby and a 3–2 win at Chelsea. I scored our first goal of the season in that opening game and was feeling pretty fit. The summer break had done me some good and, although I had to keep a constant watch on them, my old 'war wounds' were not troubling me any more than usual.

Our first 'home' game was against Arsenal and we played them at Anfield of all places. It felt odd to be sitting in the home dressing room at Liverpool's famous ground. We beat Arsenal 3–1 and then played our next 'home' game at Stoke, beating West Bromwich Albion by the same scoreline. I missed that one but I was back for the following away matches at Wolverhampton, which we drew, and then at Everton, which we lost 0–1. That defeat was significant because it was our only loss in the first 14 League matches of the season until we suffered our second defeat at home to Leeds. Even that did not stop us because we then went a further eight games without defeat and, as 1971 ended, we were serious championship contenders, having led the way for most of the season thus far.

It was too good to last of course. I think that the League Cup took it out of us a bit. We had made our exit at the hands of Stoke in the middle of November, but it had taken two replays to achieve a result. In the previous round we had beaten Burnley after a replay and, including the victory over Ipswich in the round before that, we had played six games in addition to our First Division programme, which took us to 17 matches in just over ten weeks. Our last three games of 1971 were all drawn, a sure sign that the race leaders were beginning to flag a little.

Then, at the start of 1972, we really slowed down. On New Year's Day West Ham beat us 3–0 away, and we lost successive League matches to Chelsea, West Bromwich, Newcastle, Leeds and Tottenham. From top place we slid down the table and were rapidly heading for the uncomfortable end of the First Division. Our FA Cup exploits were not so bad, though. We beat Southampton after a replay, went through at the first attempt against Preston, beat Middlesbrough after a replay and then had to face Stoke in the sixth round. Yes, Stoke again. They held us to a 1–1 draw at Old Trafford and then beat us 2–1 again in the replay. At least it had only taken one replay this time.

Our form was up and down for the rest of that season. Frank O'Farrell went into the transfer market to try to steady the ship. One signing was a failure but the other was absolutely brilliant. Ian Storey-Moore joined us from Nottingham Forest and I thought that it was a bit worrying when I saw him being strapped up so heavily around the ankles just for training. It did not send out positive messages as to his fitness, and in fact he played comparatively few games for United before being forced to retire because of his injuries. However, he was there for that season and he scored five useful goals in 11 games. They all help.

The other signing was a massive success but then, what would you expect from someone who joined the club from Aberdeen? I'm talking of course about Martin Buchan, who went on to carve out a brilliant career with Manchester United, as indeed he had already done in the years he had spent at Aberdeen. Martin later became captain of both United and Scotland and he was the first player to captain both the winners of the FA Cup and of the Scottish FA Cup. He was a tremendous player, as many long-term United fans will agree.

Despite the undoubted contributions of Ian Storey-Moore and Martin Buchan, we ended in eighth place for the third successive season. We had the satisfaction of beating Stoke City 3–0 on the last day of the season but earlier defeats by Manchester City, Liverpool and Frank O'Farrell's former club, Leicester, did not help our cause. When the season finally ended we had nothing to show for it. I had played in 32 League matches and scored 13 goals, which meant that I was second top scorer again behind George Best.

During the season John Connaughton had come into the side as goalkeeper for three games. He had been an apprentice at Old Trafford since he left school and was given his big chance when he was just about 22. We lost two and drew one of his three games for the side, and so much is expected of Manchester United players that he never played for the first team again. It seemed a little unfair that he should be asked to

172

do such a big job at such a relatively young age for a goal-keeper and then be considered a failure on the strength of those three games. Sammy McIlroy also made his début that season and went on to have a glittering career, I am pleased to say. That's football, I guess.

At the end of the season I considered asking Frank O'Farrell for a photograph of himself so that I could remind myself of what he looked like but, in the end, I thought it was probably best to keep my joke to myself as I was not in any rush to be put on the transfer list again. Anyway, the manager had much more to think about than Denis Law's sarcasm. George Best had gone walkabout in May when he was supposed to be play-ing for Northern Ireland against Scotland. He turned up in Spain and told the world that he was retiring from football. You can imagine how well that went down back home in Manchester.

The crisis was eventually sorted, and the Charlton–Law–Best trio lined up for the start of the 1972–73 season, but not before some pre-season training that would have exhausted a bunch of SAS guys. Malcolm Musgrove was a firm believer in tough training schedules and we used to have to run and run until we could all have won the gold medal in an Olympic marathon. Some people would say that he was right to ensure we had the stamina, but it is no good being a super athlete in football if you peak before the season begins and, at the same time, forget what a football looks like.

It should not have been too much of a surprise, then, that we lost our opening game, going down 1–2 at home to Ipswich. I scored our first goal of the season once again but it was no consolation. I missed the next few matches because of injury and so I take no blame for the Nightmare on Merseyside. Within four days we lost 0–2 in successive away matches at, first Liverpool, then Everton. There followed four drawn games on the trot and two defeats. It was not until 23 September 1972 that we won our first League match when we managed to beat Derby 3–0.

In a bid to add some strength to the attack, Frank O'Farrell had bought Ted Macdougall from Bournemouth, who had been a phenomenal goal-scorer for the Cherries. But getting the ball into the net in the First Division is a very different proposition, as Ted soon discovered. He played only 18 games for United, all of them that season, and he scored just five goals – which was more than I scored during the same period but was still not the answer to United's problems. Wyn Davies was another signing. He was a very good striker but he also found it a struggle to join a team in disarray.

Off the pitch the George Best saga continued. George had always had the greatest respect for Sir Matt, but he did not consider Frank O'Farrell to be in the same league. It was clear that Besty had little or no time for him. In an attempt to bring George to heel, Frank had arranged for him to live with the Crerands, but George had spent just one night there before finding other pillows on which to lay his head. A psychiatrist had been called in but that proved an absolute disaster as Best found the whole episode hilariously funny, and he and that shrink parted company with each thinking the other totally mad.

In September of that year the club staged a testimonial game for Bobby Charlton. George pulled out at the last minute and went for a drinking session instead, which led to red faces all round. I did not fall out with George. Few of us did. You could not help but like him no matter what he did. Probably the greatest excitement in the dressing room before a game was the issue of whether or not George was actually going to be there. Frank O'Farrell tried all sorts of things to discipline him but they simply did not work. George would only ever listen to Sir Matt, although he would tolerate a bit of earache from one or two of the rest of us.

We struggled in the League Cup and were taken to a replay by Oxford United before we went through to the third round and were knocked out after another replay by Bristol Rovers. I missed that game but it was still an embarrassment to be beaten at home by Bristol Rovers. Times were indeed very difficult – and they became worse.

I found myself on the bench more often than not during that season. I understood that the manager had to play his strongest side but, when I saw Ian Storey-Moore looking like a mummy beneath his kit, and the new signings faring no better than I would have done, it was a very frustrating experience. As a substitute you are usually sent on when the chips are down and everyone expects you to perform a miracle. It does happen sometimes, but it is very rare, and it does not do your own confidence any good to have all that pressure for a few minutes with only disappointment, usually, at the end of it.

Such a disappointment was our away match at Crystal Palace, who were also struggling in the First Division at that time. In the preceding few weeks we had beaten Liverpool 2–0 at home, lost at Manchester City and beaten Southampton and Norwich before Stoke defeated us 2–0 at Old Trafford. We seriously needed a victory at Selhurst Park, or at least a good performance even if the result ended up as a draw. I was on the bench again and had to sit for most of the match in sheer torment as Crystal Palace crawled all over us.

We went into the game in 20th place, one below Palace, so maximum points would have been a very nice bonus. By half-time we were losing 0–2. There was no Charlton in the side. Besty had gone walkabout and been placed on the transfer list again, then taken off again and told to resume training. However, he was not ready for that game. While Crystal Palace were not much good, we were even worse. In the second half they put three more goals into our net without any reply. I was sent on late in the game but it was all over by then and, to be honest, I don't know if I would have made much difference had I been there from the start. We were terrible and it was one of the most humiliating matches of my career – if not *the* most humiliating.

The dressing room was like a morgue. Nobody offered any argument or pointed blame at anyone else. It was dreadful, almost as if we were at a funeral. I am only glad that nobody had a cut-throat razor with them, otherwise there would have been a queue to borrow it.

The newspapers by then were serving up Manchester United stories as if there was about to be a famine. Was O'Farrell going to go? Was Best back to stay? Was the unthinkable about to happen and Manchester United be relegated only four years after winning the European Cup? If the club cat caught a mouse it became headline news. It was a reporter's paradise at Old Trafford.

Finally the volcano erupted. Three days after the defeat at Selhurst Park, Frank O'Farrell was sacked along with Malcolm Musgrove and John Aston, our chief scout. We said our farewells and I nearly had to ask someone who the chap was standing next to Malcolm Musgrove. We had never come to know each other. I don't like to see anyone sacked and I felt sorry for them as they made their exit, but I have to say that I could not give any details about Frank O'Farrell because he always remained a total stranger.

The other sensational news was that George Best had been sacked as well. The announcement stated that George had been placed on the transfer list again and would not be considered for first-team action with Manchester United. That really saddened me. How could anyone allow that sort of talent to go to waste? The club was at its wits' end and George seemed to be at the end of his wits.

Once again speculation was rife about who was going to be the new manager. It was obvious that Sir Matt was not going to make yet another come-back, although everyone would have been more than delighted if he had. We were now only one place from the very bottom of the First Division and something quite dramatic needed to happen at Old Trafford if we were to get out of trouble.

The directors obviously recognized the need for a revolution and they sent for the one man, other than Sir Matt, who might be able to pull something out of the bag. That man was Tommy

Docherty. We knew a day or two ahead of his appointment that he was going to be offered the job because Sir Matt talked to both Willie Morgan and myself about him. He wanted to know what we thought of Docherty and how we had felt playing for him in the Scotland team. We both gave glowing accounts of the man.

I had known Docherty since 1958 when I made my international début. Tommy Docherty was still a Scotland player in those days and I had seen quite a bit of him in the years that followed, even when he was no longer a part of the set-up. When he returned as manager I had enjoyed the experience and therefore I had nothing but good to say when asked by Sir Matt. The final question was whether or not Willie and I thought he would be a success as the next manager of Manchester United. We both instantly said that he would.

I saw Docherty as just the sort of rough, tough, tracksuited manager who would put the fire back into the bellies of the players. We needed leadership and he was certainly the man to provide it. As a player he was uncompromising and would tackle anything. As a manager he had proved himself to be exactly the same. On a personal note he had been very good to me when I was a young player with Scotland and he had certainly helped me settle into international football. When he became manager he also recalled me to the national side at a time when many people thought that I would never again wear a Scotland shirt.

I had good reason to be grateful to Tommy Docherty, but I put all of that aside when I recommended him. I was only interested in what was going to be good for Manchester United. The club was in despair. The team spirit was non-existent and even those not directly concerned with the football side of things had become worse than subdued. Usually, it did not matter if you were the chairman, the tea-lady or a turnstile operator, you were all members of the same family and everyone spoke to everyone else as if we were all on a permanent holiday. Now, however, it was different. Everyone brooded in their own particular corner and the club had gone from being one happy family to being a collection of individuals who lacked confidence, faith in the future, and even trust in each other. It was a dreadful environment but one that I thought Docherty could change and perhaps return to the way it had been. He had the charisma to pull everyone out of the doldrums.

Only a few days after the departure of Frank O'Farrell, Tommy Docherty, with the blessing of the Scottish Football Asssociation, was named as the new manager of Manchester United. It was the start of another new era – and the eve of the end of another.

15

ELBOWED BY THE DOC

There is no doubt that the arrival of Tommy Docherty was a turning point in our season. He set about the task in his usual rough-and-tumble fashion and I must say that he was a tremendous motivator with the younger players. Those with more experience had seen it all before and therefore were perhaps a little slower in their response, but the young lads almost believed that they could walk on water after listening to the Doc.

His first game in charge was at home to Leeds and I was back in the starting line-up for the first time in nearly two months. We were all fired up and desperately keen to get our fresh start off to a victorious beginning. We nearly did too. Ted Macdougall put us in front and it stayed that way right up to the closing minutes. I had been substituted and watched help-lessly from the bench as Allan Clarke grabbed an equalizer only moments before the referee blew the final whistle. Coming as it did after two bad defeats, we should have been happy to have steadied the ship, but we were choked because we knew that we were worth the victory and the maximum points would have been very useful.

Three days later it was Boxing Day and we were away to Derby County. I was not playing, so was left biting my nails as we lost 1–3 at the Baseball Ground. I think that defeat drove home to the new manager the immensity of the task he had so recently undertaken. He immediately dived into the transfer market and, by the time of our next match against Arsenal at Highbury, there were certainly a few changes in our line-up. George Graham had joined us from Aston Villa. It was the second time that Docherty had signed him – he had bought him for Villa when he was manager there. George made his United début at Highbury because the game scheduled before that, against Everton, had been postponed. Alex Forsyth joined us from Partick Thistle and he too pulled on a United shirt for the first time in that match, which we unfortunately lost 1–3. We had another new face on the bench, because Docherty had enlisted the aid of Tommy Cavanagh as coach. Pat Crerand, who had been put in charge of team affairs before the arrival of Docherty, was made the Doc's No. 2.

We were now rock bottom of the First Division. It seemed that United's world had been tipped upside down because it had not really been that long since we were shining at the other end of the table. At least it was no longer possible to go any lower.

When the news broke that Lou Macari had asked Celtic for a transfer we all guessed where he would be heading – and we were not wrong. Jim Holton and Lou Macari both joined the club in time for our next League match. We had been knocked out of the FA Cup by Wolves between First Division fixtures and, to be honest, while nobody likes to lose it was probably a blessing in disguise. Now that we were out of the FA Cup we were able to concentrate much better on saving our First Division lives.

We travelled to West Ham with a side that was beginning to look more like a Scottish international squad. The names of Morgan, Graham, Holton, Macari, Forsyth, Buchan and Law were all on the team sheet. I'm pleased to say that we did not lose. We drew 2–2 and, once again, it took a fairly late West Ham goal to deprive us of a victory. At least we had gained our first point of 1973.

I appeared only once more during that season, but I was well aware of what was going on. The Docherty influence was beginning to work on the pitch but there was a bit of embarrassment away from it. After playing West Ham, United met Everton in the rearranged League fixture and that match ended in a 0–0 draw. The main story of that one was that Ted Macdougall was taken off and replaced by Brian Kidd. Ted went straight to the dressing room, bathed and changed and went home before the match ended. He was not a happy man and that reflected a lot of the feelings that were beginning to creep into the dressing room. Docherty was a volatile character, and the trouble with that was that once you started to splash the water there was no doubt that you were going to get extremely wet yourself.

There was another worrying aspect. Paddy Crerand and his wife Noreen were good pals of Di and myself and we regularly used to go out for meals together – at least once every week. Paddy and I had been mates for years. Nothing about that changed but it did become a little awkward after he was made Docherty's assistant. It became even more awkward when Docherty, who was staying in an hotel in Manchester until his family could move to the area, started coming with us to the restaurants. Players very rarely socialize with managers except at official events and I found it extremely uncomfortable to be sitting at the table with my boss, who did little else but talk about football.

I was beginning to wish that we could bring our traditional restaurant outings to an end. Not because I didn't enjoy the company of our usual friends, I did, but Docherty had added a dimension that took a lot of the pleasure out of it. It was during one of those meals that something was said that turned out to be quite a disappointment. Docherty began talking about my future. The upshot was that he said he realized I did not have that many playing years left but, if I wanted it, there would be a job for me on the coaching staff at Old Trafford.

This was music to my ears because I would have been keen to stay at Manchester United for the rest of my life if only I was given the chance. I had no intention of becoming a manager but the idea of coaching appealed to me. It was an exciting prospect and I began to look forward to many more years of involvement at Old Trafford, however long or short the rest of my playing career was going to be.

Docherty later denied that he had ever made any promises, saying that he could not possibly have promised me a job for life as he did not know how long he would be there himself. You would have to be a half-wit to think that I would take a promise like that as concrete, but I did take his word that there would be a coaching job for me for at least as long as he was manager. That was not just my understanding of what he had said but also that of the others who were there at the time.

Much water has passed under the bridge since then of course, and the only reason I am bringing up the subject again is to explain how I was feeling during the months that followed. I was as keen as ever to play, but for a variety of reasons I was not in the starting line-up again that season, except for one occasion when we beat Norwich 1–0 at home. That was to be my very last competitive game for the club. I was also eager to get involved with the coaching and waited for the opportunity, but it was extremely slow in presenting itself. I guessed that Docherty had quite enough on his plate getting us out of trouble and so I did not push it.

There is no doubt that Tommy Docherty did prove to be the saviour of Manchester United – at least for that season. A run of eight games without defeat was a tremendous help and saw United climb from the bottom to just below midway in the table. And despite a few poor results towards the end of the season, it was apparent that Manchester United were not going to be relegated.

I was looking forward to seeing Manchester United being re-born and chasing the championship again the following season. The one thing I was not expecting was the fiasco that was in store for me. George Best's future was hanging in the balance, Bobby Charlton was retiring at the end of the season, but the third member of the trio – namely, me – was destined for more work in the United cause. Or so I thought.

On the Thursday before the team was due to travel to London to play Chelsea the following day, I reported to the Cliff for some light training. I was not fit enough to play in what would be the last match of the season and planned to spend the afternoon looking at some house improvements with Di, who was well along the pregnancy road at the time. Our kids were on school holiday and had been packed off to Aberdeen to spend some time with the folks.

Tommy Docherty asked me to pop into the office for a moment. What exactly he wanted me for I didn't know. I did not think he was going to ask me to travel to London because I was not fit enough, though it would not have taken me long to throw a few things into a bag if he was desperate. What I certainly didn't expect was what he said to me: 'We have decided to give you a free transfer.'

I am not often rendered speechless but that one really shut me up for a while. I simply could not believe what I had just heard. A free transfer? But what about that coaching job I had been promised? And who exactly was 'we'? Was this a decision that had been taken by the club or was this just Tommy Docherty craftily exchanging 'I' for 'we'?

He had known how things were at home and had spoken very positively to me when I had talked about a new house, even suggesting that the club might provide me with a mortgage. Now, everything had suddenly changed. My first thoughts were for my family. I did not want Di to hear all this in as shocking a manner as I had, or for the pressure and tension to affect her while she was pregnant. At that stage I was far too taken aback even to get angry. One minute I had had an exciting and secure future and the next – oblivion.

I was due a testimonial at the start of the following season to which Ajax had already agreed to come, and I was informed that it would still go ahead. My mind went into overdrive. I did not want to stop playing just like that. I knew that my injuries were a worry but I felt that I had something to offer, at least for another couple of seasons. The trouble was I did not want to be separated from my family and neither did I want to move and drag the kids away from their schools where they all appeared to be making such good progress. I did not particularly want to go down the divisions in my twilight years either. All this really meant that there was no other club that I could possibly join – unless it was Manchester City, and there was precious little chance of that happening.

I decided that the best thing I could do would be to retire from playing and I suggested, to keep everything neat and tidy, that it would be better if I remained attached to United until my testimonial and then I would announce my retirement immediately after that. It would save a lot of hassle and do away with any embarrassment or bad feeling. As far as money was concerned, my contract still had some time to run and so the arrangement I suggested would actually save United some money. Docherty was enthusiastic about my proposal and thought it was the ideal way to settle it.

With all that in mind I went home and did not say a word to anyone about the conversation that had just taken place. Docherty's last words to me were to give me permission to go to Scotland to pick the children up from their holiday. After the game against Chelsea, United were travelling to Italy to take part in a tournament and the Doc said he would see me when they got back to Manchester.

I travelled to Aberdeen, leaving Di back in Manchester. Up there, I went for a lunch-time drink with some friends, but avoided answering too many questions and talked up the future of Manchester United instead. As we sat there chatting the football news came on television and suddenly we heard the announcement that Tony Dunne and I were being given free transfers by Manchester United. The place went as quiet as the grave. They thought I had been less than honest with them and it made me feel very foolish. I was also extremely angry. After all the promises and agreements someone had 'leaked' the information – and I had a pretty shrewd idea of who that someone was.

It took only minutes for the press to track me down and begin asking their questions. What was worrying me was knowing that the same thing was probably happening back in Manchester, where Di was on her own, having to deal with the press gang unaided. I immediately collected the kids and we raced back to Manchester. The whole story had not been released, simply the fact that I had been given a free transfer. I did not enlighten anyone further and merely said that I had been happy at Old Trafford and that I had no particular plans for the future.

As soon as I had the chance I went to see Sir Matt. He tried to keep the peace by saying that Docherty had been forced into making a statement by the pressure of the press. I knew that was not true because nobody other than Docherty and myself were aware of the arrangement we had made, and there had not been time for the news to have been 'leaked' by a board member. The news had been broken quite deliberately.

There were offers from various sources. I remember Harry Gregg getting me out of the bath to offer me a place with Swansea, where he was then manager. It was a kind thought but I had to explain to him, and others, that my family mean everything to me and I did not want to have them shunted around the country just so that I could play football, nor did I want to live in digs away from them. What hurt me more than anything about the way my departure from United was handled was the pressure it put on my family for a while.

A few years after these events took place I was called to appear in a court case between Tommy Docherty and Willie Morgan. The story I have just related came out and Docherty admitted it was true. Had it not been mentioned in court I would have kept it to myself because I do not like to put my own dignity on the line just to get even with other people.

I have already said that there is no doubt in my mind that if Tommy Docherty had not joined United that season, the club would have been relegated, and he deserves all credit for the fact they were not. I know that Sir Matt Busby would not have been tempted out of retirement again and someone had to replace Frank O'Farrell. For that reason I was glad I spoke well of the Doc when I was asked about him. I did, of course, get to know him a lot better when we were working together on a day-to-day basis and I'm not sure I would have been as full of praise of him had I experienced that sort of relationship before. As managers go, he was better than some but not as good as others. He was always good for a laugh but, after a while, you came to realize that his instant wit was not quite as instant as it appeared. His gags were rarely off the cuff but very often tried and tested jokes which were always guaranteed to make him the life and soul of the party.

I do not harbour any grudges and therefore, if we meet, we speak as acquaintances – but certainly never as old friends. I know that Docherty has since given a different account of the affair, but I was there and I remember our conversations at dinner and our discussion in his office at the Cliff on that Friday morning when my United world suddenly collapsed.

I played for Manchester United for around ten years. I scored 171 League goals in 309 games and took part in cup successes both at home and abroad. I played alongside and against world-class footballers and sampled the unique joy of having a great relationship with the magnificent Manchester United supporters. I served under the greatest manager of all time, Sir Matt Busby, and I enjoyed wonderful experiences virtually every single day of my life at Old Trafford.

It was all over now, of course, and I did not think that I would ever play at Old Trafford again. That saddened me because I had not had a chance to say goodbye. When Bobby Charlton called it a day, his retirement from United had been announced in advance, and there was an opportunity for goodbyes. My own departure had not been like that and I felt cheated in more ways than one.

16

THE BITTER END

I have been asked countless times how I felt at the end of the 1973–74 season but, before I can answer the question truthfully, perhaps it is better to ask how I felt at the start of it. I was quite a happy guy actually because, within a few days of having been given the elbow by the Doc, I was back in the game and the season to follow was so crammed with drama that it is almost worth a book on its own.

Less than a week had passed when I went to the Football Writers Annual Dinner in London. It was always held on the Thursday before the FA Cup Final and I had a longstanding arrangement to attend, so I thought I might as well show my face. Early in the evening I was approached by Johnny Hart, who had taken over as manager of Manchester City, replacing Malcolm Allison. I was surprised – putting it mildly – by his third question.

'Hello, Denis, how are you?' That was the first question. A normal opening to a conversation.

'What are your plans?' That was the second question. Again, a query that was to be expected in the circumstances.

'How about playing for Manchester City?' That was the third, totally unexpected, decisive question.

I answered respectively – 'Fine!', a shrug, and 'Yes!'

In my mind, the last possibility was that I would ever return to Maine Road. But what a great prospect it was! I sat through the meal pondering on the chance of extending my playing career with the last club that I would ever have expected to join. I was so engrossed in my own thoughts that I must have been pretty poor company and I do apologize at this late date to those who were sitting at the same table. The one thing that did not occur to me was that I would be playing against United.

During that summer I bumped into many United fans and some of my former team-mates. All of them wished me the very best, which was nice, especially when you consider that I had just joined the opposition. I enjoyed the summer break, but I was keen to get back to training in preparation for the coming season. Johnny Hart was a good manager who had great empathy with all his players, and I certainly felt very comfortable back at Maine Road, even though my thoughts did often travel back to Old Trafford as I wondered how things were going there.

The new season began with a home match against Birmingham City and the team that lined up for that opening game included some really big names. Joe Corrigan was in goal and Tony Book, Willie Donachie, Mike Doyle, Tommy Booth, Alan Oakes, Mike Summerbee, Colin Bell, Francis Lee and Rodney Marsh were all in the side, with Frank Carrodus on the bench. I had been used to lining up with some of the greatest names in football while I was at Old Trafford, but I certainly could have no complaints about being in the same City side as that lot.

I could not help thinking back to my last few days at Old Trafford as I prepared to go out on to the Maine Road pitch. I was a write-off according to my previous manager. Now I had the chance to prove that I could still deliver. I scored twice as we beat Birmingham 3–1. Trevor Francis was in the visiting side and he went home unhappy that day. As for me, I was definitely 'over the moon'.

A week later we drew at Stoke and I scored our goal in that game as well. We had lost 0–1 at Derby during the week, but I was still happy with my three goals in three matches. By the time we were into the second month of the season I had missed a couple of games through injury, had become dad to our fifth child and first daughter, Diana, and had been recalled to the Scotland side after Willie Ormond came to watch me play for Manchester City. Victory over Czechoslovakia ensured Scotland a place in the 1974 World Cup and there were huge parties in Glasgow that night. I joined in for a short time, but I did not expect to be in the Scotland squad for the finals in West Germany. Manchester City had lost only three of their opening nine games and we were in a comfortable position in the top half of the First Division, so there were no complaints from me.

October also proved to be a decent month. I played for Scotland again, my club maintained their place in the table and I scored another goal. At the same time we were making progress in the League Cup, so all seemed to be going quite well. However, there had to be trouble ahead to spoil everything, and it soon arrived when it became increasingly apparent that Johnny Hart was far from well. Tony Book was taking more and more responsibility with the team and, when Johnny Hart had to leave the stadium just a few hours before we played Leeds at the end of October, it was obvious that we would soon be meeting a new manager.

It was no surprise, therefore, when Johnny Hart gave up the job because of ill health and every one of us was sorry to see him go. The day after Johnny resigned our next manager-to-be had a row at Norwich and walked out on his job. Five days later he was appointed manager at Manchester City with Tony Book as his assistant. Suddenly, I found myself with a new boss – Ron Saunders.

Ron Saunders came to Maine Road with a bit of a reputation for ruling with an iron fist. There is no doubt that he was a gritty character but I think that, at times, his image belied the real man – who was a very successful manager in later years. He adopted a more defensive style as soon as he arrived, which did not sit well with me because I had always found myself much more comfortable with the old Busby style of 'go out there, play football and score more goals than them'.

Saunders antagonized some of the more established players by continually referring to them as 'old players'. It did not bother me; I had often been called much worse than that. I am sure he meant it as a joke, but a few of City's long-term favourites became a bit fed up with it. The trouble was that with Ron Saunders it was not easy to tell what was meant as a joke and what was not.

I think he made a few mistakes during his time at Maine Road and one of them was trying to make too many changes all at once. We were going quite well in the First Division, so there was hardly any need for sweeping changes. Some adjustments would have been understandable, but not a complete change of style. I don't think that alienating the senior players was such a good idea either.

Saunders did succeed in getting us to Wembley for the League Cup Final, but in the First Division we slumped a little and our promising start soon evaporated. Within a few weeks we slipped from ninth place to a worrying 16th. Meanwhile, I found myself playing more games in the reserves than I would have liked, especially since I wanted at least a sporting chance of making Scotland's World Cup squad – a dream which grew more and more distant with every reserve game that I played for my club.

It was quite telling that the biggest First Division score we had all that season in a match was three, and that the two occasions when we achieved that were both during Johnny Hart's regime as manager. There is no doubt that the tactics adopted by Ron Saunders were first-class for some clubs – but not for us at that time. There were too many attacking players with flair at Manchester City in those days to have them wasted on a negative policy.

The League Cup Final took place at Wembley on 2 March 1974, and we were pitched against Wolverhampton Wanderers, with whom we had drawn 0–0 at Molineux earlier in the season. We were a team of walking wounded and it showed, because we never really got to grips with the game. Wolves beat us 2–1 and we trooped off a disappointed, and probably disappointing, side. The only consolation for me was the fact that if someone, some months earlier, had told me that I would be taking part in a Wembley cup final, I would have laughed at them.

The week after the League Cup Final our First Division form took a dive again. It had recovered a little during the early months of 1974, but we lost to Leeds and that put us back a bit. The next match on our agenda was the first of the local derbies against Manchester United and I was extremely disappointed when I learned that I would not be playing.

It proved to be quite a game, with tempers boiling over in every part of the pitch. Rodney Marsh, Francis Lee and I had all been dropped but, had we been playing, I don't know what might have happened. I don't think it would have made the afternoon any easier for the referee, Clive Thomas. As it was, he had to send off Lou Macari and Mike Doyle for fighting. They refused to go. There were other scuffles breaking out as the arguments raged and the referee finally took both teams off the pitch for ten minutes in order to cool everyone down. Later the game resumed without those two players. The final score was 0–0, but I think City won on points because they had only one player sent off and one booked, while United had one sent off and three booked.

I returned to the side a few weeks later but we were beaten 3–0 by Queens Park Rangers and, following that result, Ron Saunders was sacked. I did not enjoy his departure but it did mean that Tony Book took over as the boss and I believed my position was much safer in his hands because he was more of a Johnny Hart man than he was a Ron Saunders man. There had been some horrifying talk of my being sold to a smaller club, but all that went out of the window once Tony Book took charge again.

Although we were not exactly in the basement of the First

191

Division, there were not too many points between the bottom club and the safety zone and so we were not assured of survival until our last but one match of the season. Our situation had worsened after the Queens Park Rangers game because we had drawn at home to Liverpool, who had then beaten us 4–0 in the return fixture at Anfield just four days later. That result took us a few places lower in the table. It was now desperately necessary that we pull something out of the bag in our last two games to be certain of avoiding the drop.

All this time I had been keeping an eye on events unfolding at Old Trafford. I was interested to see that Docherty had persuaded George Best to try again. It did not last. George played a dozen games from October to the end of the year and then he disappeared again. That really saddened me because, just like everyone else, I knew that George was probably one of the most talented players of all time, and to see it all being wasted was dreadful.

I used to meet up with the United players and, even though they were putting on a brave face, you could see they were not at all happy with the situation. I was beginning to think that Docherty had actually done me a big favour because I was much happier at that particular time than I would have been in the shoes of those United guys, who were so obviously going through some sort of nightmare. Although I was prepared to play my heart out for Manchester City, or any other club that employed me, my love affair with Manchester United was far from over.

As I listened to their results for game after game I could hardly believe what I was hearing. From the middle of September until the beginning of March they won just two matches out of 22 First Division fixtures. Many times I had to double-check when I heard a score, because I could not come to terms with what was happening. At one stage they scored only one goal in five games. Sammy McIlroy was their top scorer with six goals. They slipped into the relegation zone on Boxing Day and stayed there for the rest of the season.

We had to play West Ham at home in our last but one game and we were keen to get the maximum points since we were almost among the contenders for relegation. The Hammers had refused to be ruffled by the threat of the drop and played their usual excellent football. On the day, however, we had the edge – or perhaps we were that little bit hungrier to be certain of retaining our First Division status. We won 2–1 and, at the same time, we could easily have done United a favour because a defeat of one of their rivals threw them a lifeline.

A scriptwriter could not have dreamed up a better plot for our last match of the 1973–74 season. It is well known now that we had to play away to Manchester United. I did not know it at the time but it was also to be my final League appearance. I could not have wished to make that final appearance anywhere but Old Trafford but, oh, if only the circumstances could have been happier.

On the day of the big game we were already safe from relegation. Some say that United were already doomed. I wish that statement were true, but the reality is that they still had a mathematical chance of staying up had the result gone a little differently. I was excited to see my name on the team sheet for the visit to Old Trafford. At first I had not wanted to play at all, but Tony Book assured me that it would be all right and that, if I were picked, I owed it to my club to play and to perform. He was absolutely right of course and I realized I had to try to look upon the match as just another fixture. Some hope of that! In the end I was looking forward to seeing the Stretford End once again, even though I was going to do my best to disappoint them.

There were some familiar faces in the United line-up. It seemed strange to me, too, to be wearing a different shirt at Old Trafford and actually playing against Alex Stepney, Alex Forsyth, Sammy McIlroy, Lou Macari, Martin Buchan, Jim Holton and Willie Morgan. A year earlier they had all been my team-mates.

It was a typical derby game with no quarter being asked or

given. We seemed to be fairly evenly balanced and it looked very much as if a draw was on the cards. United threw more and more at us as the game progressed. They needed all the points and nothing less would do. Unfortunately, as they went all out for attack they left themselves vulnerable in defence and we were able to scare them a few times.

I think there were just about eight minutes left. We were at the United end and putting them under pressure. Someone tried a clearance but the ball ran loose and a cross came over to exactly the place where I was standing just in front of the goal. Nobody had moved, so I was not in an off-side position. I did not think. I simply reacted and back-heeled the ball over the line before Alex Stepney could dive at my feet. There was no question that it was a goal, but there was no arm in the air in salute from me. I looked down at the ground and walked away.

How did I feel?

Numb, that's how I felt. I felt as though I had unwittingly seriously injured my closest friend. I think Tony Book understood because he substituted me almost straight away. It was my last kick of that season and of any other – and it had confirmed relegation for Manchester United.

I had only just got to the bench when I heard a commotion. I looked up and saw hundreds of fans running on to the pitch. It wasn't the first time there had been crowd trouble at Old Trafford and I hoped that this was not going to be one of those occasions that everyone later seriously regrets. It could have turned out very ugly and we were all concerned.

A group of United fans were running in my direction and I began to think that I was in for a bit of a hiding for scoring that goal. Then I noticed something, they were all grinning. One threw a United scarf around my neck and every one of them seemed to be wanting to shake my hand. They weren't looking for trouble at all. They had already resigned themselves to relegation and they wanted to show me that there were no hard feelings. 'You're still the King,' one of them said, and I felt a lump in my throat.

The referee, David Smith, had little choice but to abandon the match. There were nearly 60,000 people in Old Trafford that day and it seemed as if 120,000 were on the pitch.

For a while I remained stunned by what was going on. It even crossed my mind that United might have fought back and scored a couple of goals in the dying minutes but for that pitch invasion. Then I realized that it would not have made any difference because their relegation rivals had won, and that fact put paid to any chance they might previously have had of surviving.

The newspapers loved it of course. The Lawman was now the Renegade – the former United player who had killed them off. They wanted me to say I was glad I had put the final nail in their coffin and that it had paid Docherty back for the way he had treated me. That sort of talk sickened me because nothing about it was true. It was the only goal that I can ever remember wishing I had not scored. I owed it to my club and to my team-mates to score – but how I wish I had not been playing that day.

For years now I have been continually asked how I felt, and for years I have given many different answers. When the press puts pressure on you to say the things they want you to say, you can either cave in or you can put on a brave face. To some I said that it was a bit of a sickener but that I did not lose any sleep over it. To others, that I couldn't have cared less, I was just doing my job as a professional footballer. Now is probably the best time to tell the exact truth.

I did feel numb from the moment that I knew the ball had crossed the line. I felt physically giddy, l could not believe that the ball had gone in so easily, and from my foot too. I could not celebrate the goal or respond to the congratulations of my team-mates because I was dazed and could not clearly take on board what had happened. I don't think it sank in fully until after I was substituted. It was almost like a form of concussion.

After the game I did not take any part in the usual dressing room banter, my mind was much too full of what had

195

happened. I wanted to get away from everyone and lock myself into my own home. As soon as I was able I did go home, excused myself to my family for a short time and went upstairs to our bedroom.

I sat on the bed with my head in my hands and relived everything that had happened, right down to the last detail. I kept seeing faces. I saw the faces of those fans, I saw the face of Sir Matt and my mind rushed back over the years. I saw Besty baffling defenders. I saw Bobby Charlton scoring with one of his thunderbolt shots. I saw Alex Stepney and Harry Gregg flying through the air, and I saw myself spinning away after putting the ball into the net for a United goal. I heard the roar of the crowd and I saw myself with raised arm, saluting them. Then I relived the moment that my heel sent the ball over the line for a Manchester City goal only a little earlier that day.

How did I feel?

I wept.

17

A LAW UNTO MYSELF

The summer of 1974 went a long way to helping me recover from the shock of being a party to the demise of the club that had always meant so much to me. Playing in the World Cup finals was a fantastic experience that few ever achieve, and to be there for the tournament in West Germany, as it was then, was a fine way to end my career. Scotland didn't win anything of course, but we gave a good account of ourselves and were the only team of all those competing who did not suffer a defeat. We came away a happy bunch of guys with praise ringing in our ears.

At that stage I did not know that my career was over. I planned a short holiday and then a return to Maine Road for training and preparation for the new campaign. I felt in fairly good condition and did not have any problems in the run-up to the 1974–75 season. Then I found I was no longer wanted in the first team. Tony Book asked me to play in the reserves and suggested that I need not play in away games, which would make life easier for me. I am sure he had only the best of intentions but all at once I found myself being treated like an old man who could not go far without his zimmer-frame. I probably would not have minded so much if I had been asked to get involved in coaching the youngsters – but I wasn't. I was just being kept in the cupboard in case of emergencies and that was not for me at all.

On August Bank Holiday Monday I finally announced that I had come to the end of the road and officially retired as a professional footballer. There was no rift between the club, or Tony Book, and myself. I fully understood their position and they understood mine. I had always wanted to go out while I was still at the top rather than drift down the divisions, perhaps even into non-League. My last appearances were in exciting matches in the top division and then in the World Cup. I don't think that I could have done much better than that for my farewell.

As soon as the news broke I received various offers to go on playing, both here and overseas – particularly in the United States. However, I decided against it. Sometimes I think that I may possibly have been a little too hasty and could have had another season or two, but I have never been one to change my mind once a decision has been made, and I think the decision I took was right for me at that time.

There were a few hints from some people who suggested that I might become a manager. However, nobody came up with a direct offer and, even if they had, I was not interested. Being a football club manager is a definite health risk. Not only do you have all that tension as you sit on the bench watching your players not doing what you have told them to do, but there is also all that work throughout the weeks with those same players, dealing with their problems, talking to the media, travelling from game to game looking at players, being answerable to the supporters who are not aware of everything that goes on behind the scenes, and to directors who seem to know even less. I valued my family and my home life too much to want that kind of existence at that time, especially since the pay of a manager was not very good. There was little compensation for a job that was almost certainly a one-way ticket to the sack together with a lot of recriminations and depression.

That was then of course. Nowadays I have a much different view. I have seen the manager's job change beyond recognition. An increase in coaching and scouting arrangements has removed some of the pressure, and certainly the rewards for the job have increased tremendously. If I was ending my playing career now there is no doubt that I would be looking at the possibility of becoming a manager. If I had a phone call even now I would probably give it some serious consideration because I know I would enjoy the challenge of today's football, which has changed so much since my playing days. As it happens, nobody has ever asked me, so the question is purely academic.

Many players go into coaching and management when they finish playing but many more do not, which I always think is a great waste of talent and experience. Even if a player has never played in the top division and has spent his entire career in the lower divisions, he still has a lot to offer because he understands the triumphs and tribulations in that level of football. I think that is why a former international player sometimes flops when he takes over as boss of a small club. He has never experienced life at that level and therefore is simply not on the same wavelength.

If the Football Association wants to invest in the future, it could, perhaps, set aside money to pay the wages of former players who would be hired out to schools and youth clubs to coach and encourage the talent of tomorrow. By that I don't mean that they should turn up to talk and look good, but to coach just as would be done at any professional club in the country.

I had not been in retirement for very long when the offers of media work began. I often found myself sitting alongside commentators for what was the best radio coverage of football anywhere in the world. In those days there was no Radio Five Live and we were on Radio Two. I like Radio Five, I must admit, but Radio Two had more of a tradition and I really enjoyed those early days.

Gradually the radio work increased and was then added to by television. In 1978 I travelled to Argentina for the World

Cup – and that was quite an experience. It was not a great place to be Scottish at that time because the nation had great expectations and the delivery was well below what could, and should, have been achieved. It was a big disappointment because Scotland's victory over Holland in their group match showed what could be done. However, the performances against Peru and Iran had already done irreparable damage, and even that momentous triumph over the Dutch was no compensation for failing to reach the quarter-finals, which was certainly within Scotland's capabilities.

It is difficult to pick out the positives as a television commentator when you are bitterly disappointed inside at what you've just seen. I knew that there were problems off the pitch, not the least being the inadequacy of Scotland's training facilities, but you can't make a statement about things like that when you are a guest in the country. You are forced to pick your words carefully and try to remain upbeat and interested when you feel like packing your bags and going home for a game of golf.

As a television commentator I have travelled as far and wide as I did as a player. I have had the privilege of witnessing some great games and I have had the doubtful pleasure of freezing my wotsits off in some of the worst press facilities in the world. I remember being at Port Vale once to comment on a game against Manchester United. Our 'vantage point' was on the roof of the main stand, and yes, I do mean *on* the roof, a very icy roof to be precise. We felt like planting a flag when we finally got there because we were convinced that it was a greater achievement than climbing Everest. I don't think that I have ever been so cold in my entire life. Viewers must have thought there was some sort of sound interference – my teeth would not stop chattering.

On another occasion I was in Moscow with Alan Parry for coverage of the game between Torpedo and Manchester United in the UEFA Cup. It was the second leg of the tie and our 'commentary box' was a single-decker bus parked on the running track that went around the stadium. You could not see the whole pitch from the bus and so I had to keep running outside to watch the play and then dashing back inside to look at the monitors, which meant that I kept on missing bits of the action. To make matters worse it was bitterly cold, although there had been some attempt at heating the bus. As a result I was going from well below freezing to just above freezing, and at the end of the 90 minutes I felt absolutely dreadful. It didn't help matters much when the game went into extra-time and then to penalties. Luckily the penalties were at the end nearest to our bus, otherwise we would not have been able to see anything from inside. Just to put the icing on the cake, United went out. It was an experience that both Alan Parry and I have never forgotten.

Some commentators are very good at their job and there are only a few who should really be doing something else. It is a far from easy job. A good commentator has to swot up on all the players, previous meetings between the teams, where they stand in their various competitions, what games they have recently won or lost, untold information about the clubs, the grounds, the referee, the linesmen, the bloke selling hot-dogs, the chief groundsman's pet goldfish – you name it, the commentator needs to know it. When I started, Peter Jones was the commentator at most of my early games and he was a great help to me. He was very professional, an expert at his job and he could have kept up a running commentary on grass growing if he had to. He was really excellent and gently eased me into my side of things and gave me a lot of confidence.

My travels for radio have been an absolute joy and I get a great deal of pleasure from my work. I prefer radio because it is not as intense as television. That is not to say that I don't enjoy the television work, but invariably I find myself with about a minute at the start, at half-time, and at the end, in which to make some telling statement about the game. It is a rush from start to finish and, if you are not careful, you can get caught up in the verbal stampede and come across to the viewers as someone who is unable to string more than a couple of words together.

Brian Moore was another of my favourite commentators. He was always a gentleman to work with, totally dedicated to his job and bristling with an armoury of the most obscure facts. He had his favourites of course, as anyone does, and I don't think he could ever be accused of being a Manchester United man, but he was always a good commentator and remained at the top of his profession for decades.

Sometimes, when I switch on Channel Four and watch Italian football, I am amazed to hear Kenneth Wolstenholme still going strong. He seems to have been around for ever – but what quality the man has. Can anyone tell me why it took coverage of Italian football to bring him back? A commentator of that calibre should never have been allowed to slip away in the first place.

I must give away one of Alan Parry's secrets. On the football pitch the man is a thug. Sometimes during tournaments media matches are organized and I have been involved in one or two of those. I have witnessed Alan Parry in action and he will tackle and kick anything that moves. Behind that cool, calm voice there lies a demon footballer who has left his mark on fellow media men from all over the world.

I have also been involved in the MUTV project, Manchester United's own cable television channel. Granada TV are also participating and it seems to have had a successful start. My role has been to interview United players and their manager. It is a golden opportunity to sit and have a relaxed chat about football, which I enjoy more than the helter-skelter of match coverage.

Many people seem to think that too much media coverage will mean the death of football eventually. They may be right in the long term but people have been saying the same thing since television first broadcast coverage of the sport. Far from spoiling the game it has placed it in the spotlight and we have seen professional football become a growth industry as a result.

We are behind the times a little in this country because media saturation of the game has been a major part of life for some years in other countries. I can remember 20 years ago being in both Brazil and Argentina and seeing live football on just about every channel available. Television had complete control of the sport, and not only did I see referees waiting to start matches while various players were being interviewed on the pitch as they prepared for the kick-off, but I even saw a goal-scorer on one occasion being interviewed as he celebrated behind the goal seconds after putting the ball into the net. That was then, and that was in South America. It couldn't happen here, could it? . . . Or could it?

There is an old expression about he who pays the piper, and football is greatly in the debt of television, which means that anything could happen. Who would have thought only a few years ago that the tradition of Saturday afternoon football would be spread over four days to accommodate television schedules? We now have games on Friday evenings, Sundays and Monday evenings to ensure live coverage. When European football is in full swing there is hardly a day when a devotee cannot tune in to live football of one sort or another.

That sort of coverage also means that new angles and new ideas are constantly being sought. More players and former players are brought in to add to the entertainment value. Managers are interviewed at half-time both before and after they go into the dressing room to talk to their players. If anyone had predicted all that a few years ago, hardly anyone would have believed him.

In addition to my media work I am also often invited to speak at special events such as charity dinners. I am grateful I had so many great experiences in the game – and was fortunate enough to play alongside some of the greatest players who ever lived – because I am never short of things to talk about and I try to be as entertaining as possible. I don't remember having had any complaints – so far. The favourite subjects are almost always Manchester United and Scotland.

You just cannot move for football these days. Years ago you might get one or two pages of a national newspaper covering the game; today you get pages and pages, miles and miles of columns devoted to football. It often makes me wonder where all those words come from. Nowadays even the smaller clubs get the sort of coverage that, at one time, was reserved only for the biggest of clubs and advertising features football more than at any time before. Everybody wants to climb on board the soccer bandwagon: politicians are forever getting involved, butchers make sausages in club colours, magazines fall over themselves in the rush to include something to do with the game and there are several magazines and periodicals devoted entirely to football. Has the world gone mad?

No, not really. It is simply that the true value of the world's greatest game is now being fully realized. Football has a place in the hearts of ordinary people in every nation of the world, more so than any other sport, and the money men have taken it by the scruff of the neck and turned it into a highly marketable and highly profitable product. Whether or not that is a good thing depends upon your own point of view.

When I look at the rewards that football now offers to those involved, and the facilities for both the players and those who watch them, I have to take the view that it is a good thing. Possibly the gap between the haves and the have-nots of the game has widened a little, but even the have-nots seem to have more than they used to. As the gap between the élite and the rest widens further, there may have to be some radical thinking and some changes for those not in the top bracket. Perhaps there will even have to be a switch to part-time football for some who have previously been full-time professionals. Only time will give the answers to the questions that are now being thrown up, and only time will tell what must be done to keep football within reach of its roots.

For my money it is vitally important for the top clubs not to be allowed to take off like rockets and disassociate themselves from the rest of the game. I do not wish to deny them their ambitions and their huge success, but rockets have a habit of coming to a nasty end by either burning out or crashing back to the ground. I would like to see all the clubs at the various levels benefit from the boom in football's fortunes.

Everything about football is gigantic at the moment. It is Hollywood, it is pop music, it is the London Palladium rolled into one. These are very exciting times for all those concerned with the game. I just hope that those same people continue to be concerned and that the game lives on for ever as the greatest sport on earth.

As for me, I carry on happily with my media work, a Law unto myself because the decision on what time to get up in the morning is almost entirely my own. It seems like only yesterday that I announced my retirement as a player, and I still believe that I could turn up for training today and be in the team on Saturday.

The mind, they say, is willing. Shame about the flesh.

18

REFLECTIONS

I go to Old Trafford quite often to watch the games and I still have a great relationship with Manchester United. Over the years I have seen all kinds of ups and downs at the club and I am often asked how Alex Ferguson compares with Sir Matt. In a nutshell, he compares very favourably. Both men came from the same sort of working-class background in which money was hard-earned, battles were hard-fought and life was full of hardship.

The similarities between Alex Ferguson and Sir Matt are quite extraordinary. Before we even consider what Fergie has achieved at Old Trafford, it is worth recalling his career at Aberdeen, where he had the most amazing success. If anything, it was even harder for him at Pittodrie because Aberdeen were by no means the biggest club in the country. His achievements were against the odds because, by rights, nobody should fare better than Rangers or Celtic, who are by far the biggest outfits in the land.

Alex Ferguson achieved his success by moulding the right kind of squad. He was thinking along the same lines as Busby and Stein before he ever became manager of Manchester United. He knew that he had to have the right blend of youth and experience and the right approach to the game. He had to have players who could adapt and not simply perform as robots.

In eight years as manager at Pittodrie he won the Scottish championship three times, the Scottish Cup four times, the League Cup and the European Cup Winners' Cup – a fair testimony to the man's ability. That is why it was such a wise choice when United quickly signed him to replace Ron Atkinson. When you remember that Alex nearly left quite early on in his United career because success did not come quick enough, it is frightening. If Lee Martin had not scored that vital goal which beat Crystal Palace in the FA Cup replay in 1990, Ferguson might have been replaced. What a terrible mistake that would have been.

When he first came to Old Trafford he took advice from Sir Matt, who was then a director of the club. However, he had his own style and ideas and he set about repeating his performance at Aberdeen, which fitted in perfectly with the style that had been so successful for Manchester United in the past. There was already a strong youth policy but Fergie made it even stronger. He bought wisely and brought in players who could easily fit in, not just with the playing style but with the whole ethos of Manchester United.

Many people say that Fergie has a very hard streak and can be extremely cutting, but I have never heard of a player complaining about that and they are the ones who are closest to the rough edge of his tongue. I am absolutely sure that he does rave and threaten – as and when it becomes necessary – because that is a part of the job, but all the players, and especially those young ones who have come through, have paid tribute to him and the way he has helped them to improve their game and achieve their status. There is no doubt at all about his knowledge of football. He has seen it all and he has done it all and he has retained the wisdom that has been earned from experience. When he bought Eric Cantona it was a masterstroke, a brilliant purchase by an exceptional manager. While everyone else thought that he was buying trouble, the United manager knew he had bought the right man for the job. It was just as if Manchester United, Old Trafford and Eric

Cantona were made for one another. The shirt, the stadium and the player were a perfect match and played a major part in the United success story.

The biggest quest on the club's agenda is to win the European Cup again. I believe that it should already have been achieved. That is no reflection on the ability of the players, or their manager, but they have not enjoyed the best of luck in recent seasons. They often seem to hit a low in form, a high in injuries, and to be deserted by good fortune at just the wrong time. A shot hits the post when at any other time it would have gone in. A major Premiership match is played only hours before the team is due to fly out for a crucial European tie. A player gets one yellow card too many and has to sit out an important game.

Without those obstacles I am absolutely convinced that United would have won the European Cup some time within the last couple of seasons. I am equally convinced that it is only a matter of time before that great trophy is paraded around Old Trafford. It is worth remembering that when Real Madrid won it in 1998 they had gone 32 years since they had last been victorious in 1966. Their patience was finally rewarded, and I feel that the same is certain for Manchester United as they strive to bring home the big one.

In European football today, we are only a step away from the Super League that has been on the cards for some time. Attempts to introduce it through the front door have failed, but it is creeping in through the back door and it is surely only a matter of time before it happens. That raises a question about our domestic game, of course. There are already complaints about too many matches and, if our top clubs become involved in even more fixtures, something is bound to give. It could mean that the Premiership would be drastically reduced in size, or that the top clubs would be fielding what would virtually be reserve sides to compete in the major domestic competitions. Either way, it needs some close attention before a European Super League gets into full swing.

I should think that the majority of supporters would enjoy it because they would be seeing the likes of Real Madrid, Barcelona, Juventus, Milan, Borussia Dortmund and the other major European clubs on a more regular basis. The danger is, of course, that the game could be placed out of reach of the pockets of many fans if tickets and pay-as-you-view became too costly.

One worrying aspect of football today is that so many foreign players have taken up residence, temporarily at least, in our game. In the long term it must stifle the progress of our own young players. That is not just supposition, it is fact. I have seen it happen before. When I played in Italy, there was hardly a forward in the League who was Italian and, as a result, the Italian national side suffered because there were no young players coming through and gaining experience at the top level. Eventually the authorities set about amending the situation by severely restricting the imports. Exactly the same thing happened in Spain.

I am far from opposed to foreign players coming to play in Britain. They bring with them some added skills and excitement, but if left to run riot, that policy could have a devastating effect on the British game. Scotland is another very good example. Graeme Souness began importing English players when he was manager of Rangers. It made a huge difference to the Ibrox club and set them on their way to winning trophy after trophy. But it succeeded in breaking a mould because, previously, it was unheard of for English players to go and play in Scotland. It has always been the other way about.

Scottish football had seen Scandinavian players in action in earlier years but, when Souness opened the floodgates, it suddenly found itself being swamped with players from all over the world. As a direct result of that, Craig Brown now has real difficulty in finding a goal-scorer for the national side. England is but a short step away from the same sort of problem and, unless something is done to help home-grown youngsters to gain experience at the top, you can forget about any of the national sides of the British Isles bringing home the World Cup – or even the European Championship.

Perhaps success at national level is not so important to us in Britain. Football supporters here tend to be followers of their club rather than their country. At least that is the way it seems to be in England. There is a slightly different attitude in Scotland. England fans travel to see their side expecting a result, and they are far more tense about the whole thing. Scotland fans go to enjoy themselves and, if their side wins, the party has even more reason for celebration. You rarely hear of trouble involving Scotland fans on the Continent. They are loud, bawdy, and sometimes unruly, but they are just having the same fun as they would if they were down the local on a Saturday night. They don't do any harm. It is wrong to generalize about such things but there is an element of England support that does not appear to have that same intention, but seem to turn up at matches wanting to cause trouble.

Some years ago Manchester United fans had a bad reputation and, for a while, were banned from travelling to away games. There were only a few who let the side down but they earned a bad reputation for all the others and denied them the pleasure of travelling to watch United in action. They were a blemish on the good name of Manchester United, which was a great shame because United fans have always been absolutely brilliant to me personally. Even when I left the club and became a Manchester City player for a season they turned up in their thousands for my testimonial early on in the 1973–74 season. The fans could easily have turned their backs on me once I had stopped wearing the red of United and pulled on the blue of City – but they didn't.

There is something else about the Old Trafford crowd: they can be just as loud when United are losing as when they are winning. It is very easy to cheer on your team when they have the upper hand, but it is not so easy to display that same sort of loyalty when the side is playing badly. Most visiting managers love it when their players silence the home crowd, but the Old Trafford fans take a lot of silencing – and ever more may it be like that.

There is nothing to compare with the fantastic sound of tens of thousands of voices when you have just put the ball in the back of the net. That, I suppose, is why a player can get fed up playing for the reserves. He feels that he is missing out on that special atmosphere that goes with first-team football. I am grateful to have experienced the wonderful support of Manchester United fans as well as the mighty Hampden Roar.

Manchester United is as huge as ever it was, probably bigger these days than even during the heady era of the 1960s. Old Trafford has everything. The players' facilities are amazing and the supporters have every possible comfort. The Museum and Tour are magnificent and the various club shops are as good as anything you might find in your local shopping mall. The whole set-up is the essence of professionalism.

It is no good being so marvellous off the pitch, though, if there is nothing happening on the pitch. In fact, that would be a passage to disaster. It takes a lot of cash to maintain the standards that United have set and, if poor results led to a drop in investors and sponsors, the club could find itself in an awkward situation. However, that seems unlikely to happen because there is a never-ending production line of talent that continues to keep the club in contention for the top honours.

I have already paid tribute to Alex Ferguson, but just look at some of the players who have become first-team men under his guidance. Ryan Giggs is one example. What a player! We are talking world class, plus some. How I would love to see him running rings around opponents in the World Cup. David Beckham is another. He is a superb player but we have not yet seen the best of him by any means. Paul Scholes, the Nevilles – the list seems endless. Then there are the players who have been bought and have become tremendous assets to the club. I have already mentioned Cantona, but what about Dwight Yorke? He is another class act who took about five minutes to

211

make his mark and has proved a great investment. If a European Super League, or even a World Club tournament, does become a regular part of the football scene, that is the sort of combination of home-grown players and wise investments that will keep Manchester United at the top of the tree where the club firmly belongs.

The notion of a World Club Championship is not a new one. The idea of pitching the champions of Europe against the champions of South America has rarely worked in the past because it involved only two teams, playing at home and away, with all the tricks of the trade thrown in for good measure. However, as a proper tournament including a number of clubs, it would work a great deal better. I am certain that it will take off because it means more income, and money seems to count above all else in today's professional game.

I was appalled by Sepp Blatter's idea of having the World Cup every two years instead of every four. Whatever possessed the man to talk such rot? Part of the excitement of the World Cup is precisely because it happens only every four years – just like the Olympic Games. It is something that everyone experiences only so many times in their life, whether they are taking part or simply watching the games on television many thousands of miles away. To turn it into a money-spinning tournament held every two years would surely devalue its prestige.

Why, oh why must we continue to have the World Cup at the end of the season rather than just before the new one? Most of the major countries, having just completed vigorous fixture programmes, have then to send off their best players to compete in the greatest football tournament in the world. The players have just been through all the pressures of domestic competition and are jaded, often injured. What sense is there in then expecting them to play like world-class superstars? It is a bit like holding the Grand National the day after the Cheltenham Gold Cup. They don't do that to horses, yet they insist on doing it to human beings. Surely the players should be given the chance to recuperate from the season and to recharge their batteries before being asked to demonstrate their skills on the world stage? Let the World Cup be held in August. There, I have started a campaign.

It is probably about time that I stepped down from my soap-box before even my own family start to yawn. I am their official taxi driver. They seem to think that I have nothing better to do than pick up the phone to answer their call to be ferried to wherever they choose to go. Not that I really mind, you know – my family means everything to me.

My wife, Di, has supported me throughout my career and has kept me as close to sanity as I could possibly get. We still live in Cheshire and, apart from reminding me of the jobs that need doing around the house, Di enjoys walking. She walks miles and miles every day and is about the only member of the family who does not take advantage of the Denis Law taxi service. My eldest son, Gary, is involved with computer type-setting – something which I find impossible to understand but he seems to enjoy. Another son, Andrew, works at Manchester airport, while Robert is into graphic design on computers and designed the cover of this book. Iain is well into music and has provided some of the background musical effects for television programmes. My daughter, also called Di, is a press officer at Manchester United, which keeps her pretty busy.

When I am not working I am something of a bookworm and will spend hours in bookshops, and I am also still trying to improve my golf. At home, I have quite a reputation for DIY – Demolish-It-Yourself. I am very good at scraping wallpaper, breaking things and ruining the garden.

I also happen to follow football. It saddens me to see Manchester City struggling the way they have been for the last few years. While I am essentially a United man, I think it is a great shame not to see the Maine Road club up there as well. I miss the buzz in Manchester before a derby match. This is a great football city and deserves to have two clubs in the Premiership. I hope it is not too long before that rivalry is restored and the edge put back between the two clubs.

I am not the sort of person who readily dwells on the past but occasionally I will look back, and then I realize just how lucky I have been. I escaped life on the trawlers simply because I could kick a football better than other people. As a direct result of that I had an exciting career which took me to distant lands, places that I would probably never have seen as a trawlerman. I had the experience of playing football in Italy, though I wish I had been a little older when I went because I might well have made more of it. I had the privilege of lining up alongside my heroes, Di Stefano and Puskas, in a World XI. It was amazing to play with such legends, to pass them the ball and receive it back. We actually became good friends. I also witnessed some of the greatest football of all time when I saw the Brazil team of 1970 – surely the best football side ever to step out on to a pitch.

I was lucky enough to have represented my country and taken part in the World Cup, and I have played in front of some of the biggest and noisiest crowds imaginable. And then of course I had the sheer delight and privilege of playing for Manchester United and of befriending the greatest supporters in the world. I would like to take this opportunity of saying a huge thank you to all Manchester United fans everywhere for the great gift of affection that you have bestowed upon me.

May I say just one further thing. There is nothing like football. Whether you are playing for your country in front of millions of television viewers and being paid a fortune to do so, or whether you are putting your hands in your pockets and paying to play in your local park or to watch a game, please never lose sight of the fact that this game of ours is supposed to be a game of pleasure.

Just enjoy yourself – I have.